SILENT SCREAMS

GIVING VOICE TO PAIN WITH A PEN

D S Kashyap, PhD.

An empirical account of the first doctoral study on detection of child sexual abuse through handwriting.

"THE TRUTH AND MYTHS ABOUT CHILD SEXUAL ABUSE"

BALBOA.
PRESS
A DIVISION OF HAY HOUSE

Balboa Press books may be ordered through booksellers or by contacting:

Balboa Press
A Division of Hay House
1663 Liberty Drive
Bloomington, IN 47403
www.balboapress.com
1 (877) 407-4847

Because of the dynamic nature of the Internet, any web addresses or links contained in this book may have changed since publication and may no longer be valid. The views expressed in this work are solely those of the author and do not necessarily reflect the views of the publisher, and the publisher hereby disclaims any responsibility for them.

The author of this book does not dispense medical advice or prescribe the use of any technique as a form of treatment for physical, emotional, or medical problems without the advice of a physician, either directly or indirectly. The intent of the author is only to offer information of a general nature to help you in your quest for emotional and spiritual well-being. In the event you use any of the information in this book for yourself, which is your constitutional right, the author and the publisher assume no responsibility for your actions.

Any people depicted in stock imagery provided by Thinkstock are models, and such images are being used for illustrative purposes only. Certain stock imagery © Thinkstock.

Printed in the United States of America.

ISBN: 978-1-4525-8750-9 (sc)
ISBN: 978-1-4525-8751-6 (e)

Balboa Press rev. date: 02/19/2014

'TO THE CHILD WITHIN EACH GROWN UP!'

FROM DEEP WITHIN . . .

Hindu dharma (religion) teaches us that each human being has five debts that he has to recognize and repay. The first debt is to the Rishis (Sages) and the unknown authors of the Vedas (ancient scriptures that lay the foundation of Hindu religion) whose wisdom is available to us through the scriptures, the books or our teachers.

The second debt is to our Pitru (Ancestors), without whom we would not have been born and whose nurture and guidance are essential to us. The third debt is to Deva (Gods) representing various forces of nature.

The fourth debt is to Nara (the human being), because as individuals we all exist in relationship with each other. And the fifth debt is to Bhu, our mother Earth and all living and non-living beings in this world.

I feel a deep sense of humility and gratitude for being offered a perfect body, mind and intellect which is nurtured by all forces around me.

It does not really matter what your box of pain looks like, because it feels just the same. What matters really is the willingness to accept the fact that we have the power to heal ourselves and go on living. We can, at any point in time, change whatever meaning we attributed to an experience and thus change that experience totally, both emotionally and physically. This is where the healing of our silent screams could begin . . .

Devayani

CONTENTS

CHAPTER 1

INTRODUCTION

The study of child psychology has proved that many of the complex mental processes can be seen in a simpler yet more intelligible form in childhood than in adulthood. Ontogeny, which is the study of the growth of an individual, clearly views a child as a dynamic, living and growing organism. The novelty of newly emergent functions at each developmental stage across the lifespan are emphasised always, yet the above mentioned typical characteristics continue to exist. It is agreed upon by the researchers in various fields that the true understanding of human development is dependent on knowledge of the past and present, social / environmental factors that condition child's behaviour. If one desires to understand the capacities, motives and value systems of adult human beings, then it is imperative to study children and the way they are growing up at any point in time. The research indicates that there are many unresolved issues that are worthy of detailed study by scientifically trained personnel. The 'silent screams' is one such effort towards realistically gauging the dynamics of child sexual abuse.

The needs for nourishment, warmth, to escape dangerous situations and for affectionate maternal nurturance are the only four needs displayed universally by human infants at birth. Over a period of time, this primary need grows into an amazingly large collection of inter-related, complex need systems. We begin to need social, status, recognition, affection, a feeling of belongingness, security in interpersonal relationships and the like. The answer to HOW the child acquires all these needs is in the fact that the child LEARNS TO NEED those. We the adults, create social conditions around the child that are conducive for her to learn to need more and more.

If this is true, that the adults create conditions for their children to learn about various aspects of life, then it is worth pondering upon the

1

thought as to why are they seen to create more of threatening situations that invoke socially disintegrating emotions like fear, anxiety, anger, distress, jealousy and disgust?? Why is it that the children world over, especially in the 'educated and civilised' cultures are coming down with severe anxiety, depression, diabetes, cardiac disorders, respiratory disorders and many more? Why is it that the paediatric clinics are visited more frequently rather than the parks and beaches? Why do we, the adults, consider the outdoors 'unsafe' than the indoors? The outdoors are full of adults, is that why? Don't we see stranger anxiety being present and displayed by the adolescents and fully grown adults rather than only the infants from 6 to 12 months? Why have we given rise to distressful environments for our own children to grow up?

Research suggests that Child sexual abuse is a distressful occurrence across all the sections of every society. It is also well known that abusive experiences can affect child's personality to a great extent and change the quality as well as direction of personal growth in future.

Life is a paradox!

14th November. The children's day, which is celebrated with such joy, enthusiasm and hope year after year and just five days later, on *19th November*, we observe the World Day for Prevention of Child Abuse. Ever wondered how we, the adults, justify both?? Each adult is born a child, exhibiting the universal need for love, protection and is identified as a child till the age of 18 years. What, then, happens to a vast majority amongst us while growing up that we seem to be totally disconnected with this fact after crossing over to the next stage of development? And one never ceases to wonder as to what happens to that child inside us? Why is it that there are so many childish people, but very few who are 'childlike'? Those childlike people, who are able to perceive what a child sees, feels and understands . . ., those who are able to communicate with a child by getting at the same level as hers, those who can empathise with her tender mind full of optimism, hope, joy, fears, hesitation and vulnerability. When do we change tracks from being vulnerable to making others vulnerable? How do we start dominating the weak ones?

2

What is it that makes one so insensitive that one indulges in abusive acts that hurt the body, mind and soul of a growing child?

What is child sexual abuse?

Child sexual abuse is the sexual use of a child by someone with more power. There is no universal definition of child sexual abuse. A few of them have been cited in this book for the reader's to glance at the vast range of conditions encompassing this issue. A central characteristic of any abuse is the dominant position of an adult, enabling him or her to force or coerce a child into sexual activity.

Child sexual abuse is the actual or threatened physical intrusion of a sexual nature, whether by force or under equal or coercive conditions (Save the children.org.uk, 2008).

The UNICEF (1998) has affirmed that this phenomenon exists in all countries, although with differing intensity and characteristics.

Child sexual abuse may include fondling a child's genitals, masturbation, oral genital contact, digital (finger) penetration, and vaginal and anal intercourse. It is not restricted to physical touch. Such abuse could include non-contact abuse, such as exposure, voyeurism and child pornography. Child sexual abuse is any misuse of a child for sexual pleasure / gratification.

The sexual abuse may begin with kissing or fondling, and progress to intrusive sexual acts such as oral sex and vaginal / anal penetration. It may be combined with emotional abuse that destroys child's self-respect that seems too difficult to retrieve back.

It is important to note that all forms of sex with children below the age of consent are illegal. A child cannot be considered to have voluntarily taken part in a sexual act and all forms of penetrative acts with a child have to be considered as rape.

This problem continues to be one of the most devastating of contemporary issues.

The theoretical perspectives and reality

Many different theories have been put forward to explain the cause and the incidence of sexual abuse. Understanding WHY somebody abuses the other person is critical for the development of any effective preventive and intervention program. Since there are no specific theorisations regarding why or how child sexual abuse takes place, researchers most often base their arguments on the following theoretical approaches meant for women. Some of the major theoretical approaches are as follows:-

1. **The victim precipitation approach:** This approach considers offenders and victims as mutually interacting partners where the victim, through signs, eye contact, gestures and words, or by being present at certain venues or being out alone at times encourages sexual assault and rape. Things like accepting a ride back home, responding in a too friendly manner in conversation, accepting a dinner invitation, visiting a male friend at home or inviting a male friend into her home may be misread or intentionally rationalized by the perpetrator as a sign of consent to sexual intercourse. In other words, a woman is raped because she failed to accurately communicate her desire not to have sex.

This theory has three main limitations. Firstly, it is one more theory, which blames the victim, understating the role of the abuser, therefore falsely attributing responsibility for sexual assault. Secondly, it fails to take into account the fact that there is no equality between an offender and the victim. It also presupposes that men must have the right, in certain circumstances, to force a woman to have sex against her will.

Myths, which derive from this approach, are as follows.

*   Women ask for it.
*   Only young and stereotypically attractive women are raped.

- Women can avoid being raped by not walking down the streets alone at nights, by wearing modest clothes etc.

2. **The family dysfunction approach:** This particular approach focuses on the family unit in contrast to the psychoanalytic model, which focuses on the individual psyche as the cause of abuse. It has become one of the most widely used explanations for the manifestation of incest and has been adopted by many government and statutory authorities in Australia, the US and the UK.

In this view, incest is seen as an overall symptom of family maladjustment. It also proposes that all members of the family are responsible for causing it to occur even though apparently uninvolved, in particular the mother of the victim. According to the approach, incest takes place in a family, which does not conform to socially approved goals or values and where, normal family hierarchy based on age and sex has been destroyed. In a dysfunctional family, incest is used to reduce tension and maintain balance within the family while ensuring that the family's pathology is kept a secret.

In this view the mother is seen to have failed fundamentally. Firstly, she is seen as a dysfunctional wife who does not fulfil her assigned role as sexual provider for the husband, or her nurturing role as mother and protector of her child. She does this by setting herself either emotionally or physically distant from the children by working outside of the home, pursuing outside interests and activities, or through illness, hospitalization, escaping into depression, or by the emotionally and / or sexually frigid.

Secondly, this view assumes that the mother's failure to provide adequate nurturing makes the love starved child accept the sexual advances of the sex starved, seductive father as a substitute for the mother's love.

Thirdly, both the mother and father are seen as dysfunctional adults who seek a role reversal and disintegration between generational boundaries with the child, cast in the role of satisfying sexual needs of the father while assuming a protective role towards the mother. The mother supposedly engineers the incestuous relationship by placing enormous responsibilities on the child such as housework, childcare and wifely duties towards her father. Thus, in this view, the mother is the real abuser. Despite its wide acceptance, the family dysfunction model suffers severe limitations.

Other than incest, this theory has little power to explain the intra or extra familiar sexual abuse and therefore fails to account for two-thirds of all of child sexual abuse. It distracts from the painful and often devastating effects incest has on the child. This approach denies who the abuser actually is. It is argued that the husband gets confused when a daughter contributes to household duties because he is used to imposing his sexual demands on whomever the house work does and he does not really notice who it is. The research has shown that 73% of mothers do act when incest is disclosed and 60% take immediate preventive action. This is in direct contrast to what family dysfunction theory proposes to be the case.

3. **The psychoanalytical approach:** The earliest proposed explanation for the occurrence of sexual abuse was Freud's psychoanalytical theory. The theory derived from his clinical work with female clients who would disclose childhood sexual abuse, often at the hands of their fathers. Freud was the first one to postulate that the trauma of childhood sexual abuse resulted in later psychic damage. This was the basis of his "seduction" theory, which he presented along with detailed case studies at a major forum in 1896. The idea that fathers were sexually abusing their daughters caused such an outrage in conservative 19th century Vienna that Freud was ridiculed and shunned by his peers. Freud argued that it is the inability to successfully resolve the psychosexual stages of development that give rise to the psychic damage he observed in his clients who had reported child sexual abuse.

Herein, the Adult sex offenders are viewed as pathologically disturbed and sexually perverted people as a result of poor psychosexual development. The distortions in the offender's psychosexual development are seen as a result of failure in his mother's parenting.

The approach explains incest in a way that normalizes sexual acts between parents and children by seeing them as natural rather than abusive and places the responsibility clearly on the child "victim ". Here again, the mother has been held responsible for the occurrence of incest and the central idea is that the child has natural affection needs, which are not met by the mother. The mother is seen as cold and rejecting and the child would turn to the father as a source of security and affection through sexual affinity.

The major limitation of this approach is that it places blame firmly on the child or the mother, and not on the abuser. Another shortcoming is that the psychoanalytical theory views most sex offenders or rapist as disturbed individuals even though the vast majority is free of any mental illness. Unfortunately, this particular approach has also led to the development of numerous assumptions that would perpetuate the conditions for victimisation of children. Some of the myths include:-

- Women want to be raped.
- Children lie about incest.
- Children are sexually provocative.
- Men who commit incest are mentally ill.
- Rapists are sex starved mad men.
- Incest is not harmful.
- Mothers encourage incest.

4. **The feminist approach:** With the emergence of the women's liberation movement in the 1960's and 1970's, people began to tell of their experiences of sexual abuse and so more accurate identification of the problem became possible. This brought in a new approach of victim centred awareness and prompted investigations to address the key issues of sexual abuse. In particular, why is it men who rape? And, why is it women and children who are primarily the victims of sexually abusive behaviour? The feminist approach is a

sociological analysis, which over the past five decades has focused on two important and previously ignored aspects of sexual abuse:-

• The unequal power relationships between men and women and adults and children. The fact that men are socialized to desire sexual partners who are younger and smaller than them explains the beliefs upon which our socialisation processes are founded.

• The abusers' responsibility for initiating or maintaining sexual abuse. So far, it is the most adequate explanation of the motivation and incidence of sexual abuse. This approach brings about the complex interplay between existing social structures, conventional attitudes and socialization. The research has overwhelmingly demonstrated that sexual abuse is not the problem of individual pathology occurring between pathological men and seductive children/women. Instead, it shows that sexual abuse is an extension of the current legal, social, economic and political systems in which we live, which manifest and reinforce male dominance over women and children.

The role of pornography in perpetuating and legitimizing child sexual abuse is also explained by this approach. The increased incidence of child sexual abuse demonstrates that not only do men exert sexual power over children, more fundamentally they find them erotically desirable. It proposes that sexual abuse is a function of masculine socialization and not a problem of parenting, which is supported by powerful evidence, gathered in last five decades.

5. **Psychological approach:** Psychological approaches to what causes the sexual abuse have focused on the abuser rather than on the victim or the family. Psychologists have focused their attention on two levels:-

• Identifying a personality profile of sex offender.
• On isolating the motivations of abusers.

This particular search for personality profiles of sex offenders has focused on establishing the personality traits that are predictive of sex offenders. A range of studies of diverse population samples have identified personality characteristics like social introversion, feelings of inadequacy and the need to exercise a high level of dominance and control in family relationships. In terms of motivation for sexual abuse, a common finding has been that alcohol or alcoholism contributes to a reduction in internal inhibitions to commit sex offences or incest. Poor impulse control is also seen as a common problem. One major limitation of this particular approach is that the evidence is contradictory and inconclusive. This view also reinforces the myth that men cannot control their sexual urges.

6. **The four preconditions model:** To bridge the gap between psychological and sociological interpretations of child sexual abuse, in 1984 Finkelhor proposed a multi-factor model, which has explanatory power on both levels. He developed a hierarchical model, which included individual factors related to the victim, abuser and the family as well as social and cultural factors. This approach can accommodate new research to enhance our understanding of why sexual abuse occurs. The model accounts for both intra-and extra familial sexual abuse. This perspective clearly places responsibility on the abuser. Following are the four preconditions for sexual abuse that come into play in a logical sequence.

   • **Motivation:** The potential abuser needs to have some motivation to abuse someone sexually. These could include emotional congruence, in which sexual contact with a child satisfies profound emotional needs; sexual arousal, in which the child represents the source of sexual gratification for the abuser and blockage, when the alternative sources of sexual gratification are either not available or are less satisfactory.
   • **Internal inhibition:** The potential abuser must overcome internal inhibitions that may act against his motivation to sexually abuse. No matter how strong the sexual interest in

children might be, if the abuser is inhibited by taboos then he will not abuse.

- **External inhibition:** The potential abuser must overcome external obstacles prior to sexual abuse. They may include family constellation, neighbours, peers and societal sanctions as well as the level of supervision a child receives. External inhibitions are easily overcome if the potential abuser is left alone with an unsupervised child.
- **Resistance:** The potential abuser has to overcome the child's possible resistance to being sexually abused. Abusers may sense which children are good potential targets, who can be intimidated or coerced to keep a secret or otherwise manipulated.

The main limitation of this particular model is that it is essentially a descriptive framework, which incorporates a range of dissonant theories and observed clinical data. Also, it cannot be viewed as a theory until it is tested empirically on a substantial group of people, in particular in its application to treatment and prevention.

These different perspectives help one realise the multilayer dynamics that affect children's lives across the globe.

CHAPTER 2

PROFILE OF PERPETRATORS (ABUSERS) AND THE SURVIVORS (ABUSED)

C hild sexual abuse affects people from a wide variety of backgrounds. The statistics show that child sexual abuse crosses boundaries of race, class, culture, ethnicity, gender, and sexuality. There is no one kind of community where child sexual abuse happens, no one type of person it happens to. Child sexual abuse affects boys, girls and trance-gendered youth. While victims and offenders are most directly affected, families and communities are also deeply impacted since there is no adequate response to the issue.

There are four categories of child sexual abuse in order of frequency as follows:

1. Inter-familial abuse (parents, siblings, cousins, uncles and aunts)
2. Extra-familial abuse (close acquaintances, neighbours, servants)
3. Institutional abuse (residential schools, clubs, training) and
4. Stranger abuse.

What kind of people would commit such an act??

1. **Paedophiles** - a person who is sexually attracted only to children. These **fixated** abusers have been conditioned from childhood and adolescence to be primarily sexually attracted to younger children.
2. **Child Molesters** - a person who has already established "normal", "socially approved" sexual relationship with adult partners and at the same time, indulges in sexual acts with children. These are also known as the **regressive** abusers, who abuses in response to stress that adds on to his existing feelings

of inadequacy and normal impulse control, thereby allowing abuse to occur.

One very pertinent aspect of child sexual abuse that we have to remember is the fact that abusing a child is not to satisfy one's sexual needs. Child sexual abuse is not about sexual gratification at all. It is about the desire to be in a powerful situation and the need to humiliate the other being. The need that has arisen out of his/ her past experiences where he/she was not in a position to stop an adult misbehaving, any which way, and feeling humiliated oneself.

What are they like?

1. Most abusers, the world over, are men; though women can also be abusers.
2. They do not belong to any particular socio- economic class.
3. Education or lack of it, does not define abusers.
4. They may or may not have any clinically defined emotional or psychological problem.
5. They can be married happily and have their own children.
6. They may or may not have history of childhood sexual abuse.

And what about the children who get abused?

Though all children are vulnerable to abuse, certain factors put some of them at risk more than others. The factors include:

1. Belief that respecting an adult means unquestioning obedience to authority.
2. Lack of appropriate sex education.
3. Social norms that give children lower status than that of adults.
4. Childs' predisposition to love unconditionally and trust implicitly.
5. Desire to please an adult.

6. Values stressing family honour.
7. Disability related dependence on an adult.
8. Dysfunctional family.
9. Low self-esteem of the child.
10. Social isolation / having few friends to share thoughts, feelings and experiences.

Child's behaviour as an indication of sexual abuse: There are various behaviours that could be seen as indicators of child sexual abuse. Some of the most prominent ones are stated as follows.

1. Sexual knowledge that is explicit or unusual / inappropriate with age.
2. Being aware of other's sexuality.
3. Sex related words or experimentation.
4. Loss of appetite.
5. Unexplained bruises or injuries in/around genital areas.
6. Anorexia.
7. Added other stress related disorders.
8. Evidence of alcohol or drug abuse.
9. Frequent nightmares.
10. Unexplained gifts in Child's possession.
11. Extra money in Child's possession
12. Pornographic material in child's possession.

Why do children find it difficult to report the abuse? While a small percentage of children report about abuse when it happens, others find it very difficult to tell because of a number of fears they hold in their minds that accompany disclosure. These fears are explained ahead:

- **Fear of remembering:** Sexually abused children often cope by pushing the fears as far back in the minds as they can, to "forget" and avoid feeling hurt again.
- **Fear of losing love:** Children often feel responsible for what happened to them. They worry that their parents and friends

will stop loving them once they know about the abuse and this particular fear of separation from loved once inhibits them from reporting the account.

- **Feelings of shame and guilt:** Children know instinctively and can sense that their sexual experience with adults is inappropriate. Abuse makes them feel "dirty". Older children have also been known to suffer from a sense of guilt than younger children.

- **Fear of not being believed:** Children fear that they will not be believed when they disclose the experience and therefore feel helpless. Furthermore, many people tend to believe that children lie and make up stories about abuse (false memory syndrome). On the contrary, the evidence suggests that children are almost always speaking the truth when they disclose abuse.

- **Fear of being blamed:** Children fear that they will be blamed for any kind of sexual activity. Abusers often make the excuse that the child "asked" to be touched sexually. Children ask for attention and affection, which is their right, and not for sex about which they do not as yet have an appropriate context for consent.

- **Fear of further harm**: Abusers often threaten to harm the child's family as a means of maintaining control. This is how the child carries the burden of keeping her family safe by not disclosing the abuse.

- **Lack of sexuality education:** This is a very important factor that keeps the children from disclosing the abuse. Their lack of vocabulary of the private parts and the resulting inability to describe acts of sexual abuse has to be paid more attention to. Children are usually not told the correct names for the private parts, and are told that "nice girls and boys" don't use such words that refer to private body parts.

Though the above mentioned reasons become barrier to reporting abusive incidences for children experiencing it, with awareness programs and many govt as well as non govt agencies approaching children by creating a safe enough environments for them to disclose, the outcome is better reporting. Hope the number of children reporting abuse increases enough for the law and order agencies to take stern action and to deter the perpetrators from committing such ghastly crime in the near future.

CHAPTER 3

A WORLD VIEW OF CHILD SEXUAL ABUSE

A s defined by the WHO (World Health Organisation), child sexual abuse is the involvement of a child in sexual activity that he or she does not fully comprehend, is unable to give informed consent to, or that violates the laws or social taboos of society.

'No one to turn to" is a report published by 'Save the Children' organisation in the UK. It is an eye opening and moistening account of what's going on in the countries around us. It discusses the scale of CSA, the under reporting and the flaws in the prevalent systems. Children as young as 6 yrs were found to be trading sex with international peace keepers and aid workers in exchange for food, money, soap and luxury items like mobile phones. This study was conducted in one of the war stricken countries. It suggests that already vulnerable children are particularly at risk of child sexual abuse. It brings to the fore three important gaps in efforts to curb abuse. The first one says that the communities lack support to children and youth. The second gap exists in the international collaboration on regulations and personnel and the third one is the lack of investment in tackling underlying causes of CSA.

The global prevalence of child sexual abuse has been estimated at 19.7% for females and 7.9% for males, according to a 2009 study published in *Clinical Psychology Review* that examined 65 studies from 22 countries. Using the available data, the highest prevalence rate of child sexual abuse geographically was found in Africa (34.4%). South Africa has the highest rates of child sexual abuse, baby rapes and maltreatment. The reason behind is the belief that the HIV virus infection is cured by having a sexual intercourse with a virgin. Due to this belief, not only locals but also foreigners flock the continent and as a result, 40,000 children get infected each year with HIV in South Africa.

Europe showed the lowest prevalence rate (9.2%); America and Asia had prevalence rates between 10.1% and 23.9%. *Though, it would be worthwhile to take a pause here and ponder on this statistics. Most of the paedophiles and molesters from Europe, come to the Asian countries to commit this crime, aren't we aware of this fact??*

In the past, other research has concluded similarly that in <u>North America</u>, approximately 15% to 25% of women and 5% to 15% of men were sexually abused when they were children. Most sexual abuse offenders were acquainted with their victims; approximately 30% were relatives of the child, most often brothers, fathers, uncles or cousins; around 60% were other acquaintances such as 'friends' of the family, babysitters, or neighbours; strangers as offenders were in approximately 10% of child sexual abuse cases. Most child sexual abuse was committed by men; studies show that women commit 14% to 40% of offenses reported against boys and 6% of offenses reported against girls. Most offenders who sexually abuse prepubescent children are <u>paedophiles</u>, although some offenders do not meet the clinical diagnostic standards for the same.

- On the whole in the United States, 1 out of 4 girls and 1 out of 6 boys is sexually abused. 70 to 73% of abusers report experiencing abuse in their own childhood. It is estimated that less than half of the assaults on children are reported to the police.
- The United States has the worst record in the industrialized nation – losing five children every day due to abuse-related deaths.
- The generally lower rate for male abuse being reported may be due to the fact that the boys are taught to be strong and competitive and the social expectation that if they cry or complain, they are less of a man.
- According to the WHO, an estimated 100-140 million women and girls around the world have forcibly undergone genital mutilation, including 92 million in Africa.

- Children living with a single parent or a parent living with an unmarried partner are most at risk for maltreatment.
- Only a fraction of abusers are caught and convicted for this crime world over. Out of those who are caught, most are released back into the community due to some reason or the other.
- There is a clear link between possession of child pornography and the actual violation of children. It is one of the fastest growing industry and many missing children are seen on these sites by the officials.
- The researchers have found that women who experienced abuse in childhood more than once, have 62 % greater risk of heart failure compared to other women. Much of the risk was related to coping strategies such as alcoholism, overeating and drug abuse.
- Bachcha Bazi, a custom prevalent in Afghanistan, is about buying young boys from poor families, forcing them to dress like women and dance in front of men before being taken for sexual slavery.
- Child marriages are legal in some countries. In Saudi (2010) a 12 year old girl died from internal bleeding following intercourse. It is not uncommon in Saudi Arabia for a 12 year old girl to be married to an 80 year old man.
- According to WHO, India has the world's largest number of sexually abused children, with a child below 16 years raped every 155th minute, a child below 10 every 13th hour and one in every 10 children sexually abused at any point of time.

In India, **The first** ever National Study on Child Abuse in April 2007, covering 13 states in India and a sample size of 12,446 children was released by Minister for Women and Child Development showing the stark reality figures:

- More than 53% children report facing one or more forms of sexual abuse.

- Almost 22% faced severe sexual abuse, 6% sexually were assaulted.
- 50% of sexual offenders were known to the victim or were in positions of trust (family member, close relative, friend or neighbour).
- Onset of abuse is from 5 years of age.
- Boys were equally at risk as girls.
- Severest sexual abuse in age group of 11-16 years.
- 73% of sexual abuse victims were in age groups of 11-18 years.

Statistical assumptions and social reality

Statistics is the study of the collection, organization, analysis, interpretation, and presentation of data. There happens to be a notion among researchers that "one can prove anything with statistics." There is also a rampant misuse of this mathematical science that misleads masses to believe something away from the reality. I think, the gap is created by the fact that it extrapolates inferences about a large group (a particular population) based on observations of a smaller subset of that group (a sample). In order for this method to work correctly, firstly, the sample must be really representative i.e. similar to the target population in all. Secondly, the validity of a statistical procedure depends on certain assumptions it makes about various aspects of the problem. If, in case, there happens to be less clarity about the statistical procedures to be applied, then the results could be far away from the reality.

Difficulties of conducting statistical studies on sexual abuse

Sexual abuse is one of the most sensitive topics for research. Neither physical mutilation, nor genocide, nor murder can evoke as strong emotions, denial, shame or dissociation as child sexual abuse can. Justices issued ban on reports disclosing that a child was raped, sodomized, sexually abused or molested, but the same judges do not object to reports about murder, mutilation, kidnapping or enslavement.

Because of these facts, all questionnaires regarding child sexual abuse, that have been given to the general population always seem to have produced extremely skewed results. In many cases, the field personnel were unable to evaluate the answers of the question the subject has given, because the methods of measurement allowed only three answers i.e. yes, no and don't know. Giving such a "black or white" question is an exercise in futility.

So long as Child Sexual Abuse is concerned, the available statistical figures are not only controversial but the incidence and prevalence of child abuse is disputed by some experts. Incidence refers to the number of new cases each year, and prevalence to the percentage of people in a population who have had such experiences. Why would this happen? The answer lies in the fact that even the most objective scientific research is imperfect. It is extremely important for the researchers to incorporate at least one or two methods used in any study that are based on opinions and judgements, not just facts and logic. And consider the fact that even the objectively best methods available still have limitations. For example, there are controversies about how to define abuse. The definitions of abuse used in official government studies are based on laws of that country, because government definitions are needed for more than research purposes. They are also needed for determining whether or not suspected abuse should be reported, investigated, "substantiated" (as actually having occurred), and lead to action by the court. In contrast, independent researchers can use different "operational" definitions because they have different purposes than government agencies, like understanding the different effects of mild and extreme emotional, physical, and sexual abuse. No matter what kind of study it is, small changes in definitions can result in big differences in statistics on sexual abuse. Another example would be the number of questions a researcher asks his participants about possible sexually abusive experiences in childhood, influences how many of those participants who were actually abused will remember and report it. Some people might need more and different cues than others, to recall similar experiences. This is why, large epidemiological studies with thousands of research subjects, but few questions asked, will always yield underestimated abuse rates.

Therefore, we have got to keep in mind that emotional and moral commitments influence everyone's reasoning and judgement to some extent. Every scientific study, and every statistic, is partly a product of biases. The results of many well constructed meta-analysis studies confirm that CSA is a global problem of considerable extent, but also show that methodological issues drastically influence the self-reported prevalence of CSA. **A new qualitatively different approach needs to be chosen to obtain the real prevalence of child sexual abuse.**

CHAPTER 4

EFFECTS OF CHILD SEXUAL ABUSE

The effects of sexual abuse on a child are all pervading, intrusive and long lasting. They cause damage at various levels of being- such as physical, psychological, emotional and spiritual. The growth and development of children having experienced sexual abuse is affected negatively without exception.

To elaborate how such an incidence can actually change the child's entire lifespan, some of the prominent effects of sexual abuse are mentioned ahead. They include Post Traumatic Stress Symptoms wherein the child experiences sudden flashbacks. Cognitive distortions that make them feel helpless under all circumstances, emotional distress where they suffer from depression, panic disorder, obsessive-compulsive disorder, aggression, and chronic irritability. These children experience an impaired sense of self and have difficulties with self protection, hence continue to get victimised. Some of them may indulge in dangerous (self destructive) yet 'tension reducing' activities like alcoholism, overeating, indiscriminate sexual behaviour and self mutilation. One effect that has been found across the globe is having difficulties in interpersonal relationships. They could become '*avoidant*' type of a person marked with low levels of inter-dependency, self disclosure and warmth or could become '*intrusive*' by being excessively demanding and controlling.

Experiencing sexual abuse in childhood has an impact on child's hormonal secretions and there are visible changes taking place in her body. Let's have a look at such physiological changes here.

- Moles are found in people who live under constant stress. They are swimmers, gymnasts, figure skaters, tennis players, gamblers and other competitive people. An average person has up to 20 moles in adulthood. This is uncommon in children and those children who have had repetitive episodes of severe trauma have more moles. The high extent of moles can probably be found in South East Asia, Japan, China and Philippines.

- The occurrence of freckles often indicates a compromised immune system. Within weeks or months of abuse, sometimes overnight, they cover a child's face and body significantly.

- 5-10 per cent of European and North American children, who are sexually abused, are seen with very large / thick eyebrows or other uncommon facial hair growth. It is also often noted in the Middle East and Central Asia.

- Childhood abuse has profound impact on the emotional, behavioural, cognitive, social and physical functioning of children. Developmental experience is detrimental to normalcy therefore; adverse events can have a tremendous negative impact on the development of the brain. McLean hospital (USA) researchers have identified four types of brain abnormality linked to childhood sexual abuse and neglect, providing the first comprehensive review about the multiple ways in which abuse can damage the developing brain. The studies show that childhood maltreatment may produce changes in both brain function and structure. A child's interactions with the outside environment cause his connections to form between brain cells. Then these connections are pruned during puberty and adulthood. So whatever a child experiences, good or not so good, helps determine how his brain is wired. The changes that take place during stressful events are permanent.

- Evidence suggests that incest leads to different illnesses in different races around the world. Sexually abused black people are much more likely to develop sickle cell anaemia and similarly; white people around the world develop leukaemia due to sexual abuse in childhood.

- Whenever there is a real or perceived threat to one's existence, the endocrine system is the quickest and the first one to respond. The Epinephrine (the emergency hormone) a powerful heart stimulant is secreted by the adrenal glands. These glands play a key role in the human body's alarm system and the hormones released by them make the heart beat at an increased and irregular speed. It also helps the lungs to take in more amount of air (hyperventilate). These hormones also constrict certain blood vessels so that blood pressure rises. There are other severe effects like unusual fat deposits and a "moon" face. Osteoporosis, peptic ulcers, diabetes, high blood pressure and slow wound healing too fall into the same category. The most serious ones include, suppressed immune system inviting infections to invade and debilitate the body, because of the absence of inflammation and other warning signals as well as mental disturbance, ranging from mild euphoria to actual psychosis. The studies have shown that sexual abuse compels the body to respond to this profoundly stressful situation, as if it is handling a life-threatening situation. It changes body's functioning within seconds.

- Children with PTSD may present with a combination of problems including passivity, distractibility and attention problems (due to hyper alertness), emotional numbing, social avoidance, dissociation, sleep problems, aggressive play, school failure and regressed or delayed development.

- Post-Traumatic Stress Disorder (PTSD) is something of an invisible epidemic. The events underlying are often mysterious and always unpleasant. It is certainly far more widespread than most people realize. *And a prime cause of PTSD is sexual abuse in childhood.*

- Recent studies have suggested that lesbian and bisexual women may be more likely to be the target of maltreatment and violence in childhood and adolescence, compared to heterosexual women. They also exhibit health conditions such as higher basal metabolic index, greater alcohol and tobacco use, and increased depressive symptoms.

Social consequences of sexual abuse

It is rather interesting to see how the effects of childhood sexual abuse on an individual, magnify and penetrate the entire society over a period of time.

Adolescents who experience abuse tend to get married and have children at a younger age than the general population trends. They also tend to drop out of the school or avoid higher education, fear independence and seek deviant peers. Following are a few of other traits that show up commonly in the behaviour of sexually abused individuals.

1. Pretence
2. Theft
3. Fraud
4. Robbery
5. Rape
6. Murder
7. Smoking, drugs, gambling, exhibitionism, orgies, promiscuity and other addictions.
8. Consumerism
9. Indifference towards crime
10. Unwillingness to punish criminals
11. Struggle for monetary gain, fast pace of life
12. Carelessness toward the future
13. Personal wealth valued more than health
14. Self destructive behaviour
15. Continuation of getting victimised
16. Strong dependence in the supernatural.
17. Misdirected anger shown in various ways such as road rage, school killings, joy killings, wars and general aggression.
18. Taking advantage of those who trust. Common examples are police committing murders and rapes, teachers and camp counsellors raping children, judges defending rapists, doctors raping the patients, presidents committing mass murders, and preachers raping the children and nuns.

Vicarious trauma and indirect effects of abuse

The threat of sexual abuse is pervasive to all the girls. Girls often know about it from the family members and friends. The effect of sexual abuse serves to increase the power of men over women and to create women who simultaneously fear men, over value and over idealize men because of their immense power, and hence remain dependent on them.

Perhaps a large number of girls have not been abused themselves but have witnessed abuse to another person such as a sibling, parent, relative, or friend. They may simply know that as girls they are vulnerable too. Such vicarious trauma will probably not cause fragmentation that may be generated in the victims, but it can create tremendous fear. Just as the trauma of the Holocaust has been transmitted inter generationally, the trauma of child sexual abuse may possibly be passed on as well.

When mothers warn their daughters to look after their own safety, and avoid the danger of getting sexually abused by men, some of the mother's anxiety and apprehension is transmitted to the daughter as well. If the mother had been subjected to the childhood trauma, the daughter is perhaps subject to a replication of the post-traumatic response, despite the warning. The warning may have carried with it the additional message of futility of struggle, confrontation and self-defence. One cannot deny the contribution of the visual media and all the violence / abuse shown constantly, in the development of the vicarious trauma. This projection of assault on the female body, by any and every male, is bound to create tremendous pressure on a growing girl, and load her with the feelings of guilt, fear, awkwardness, shame, pessimistic outlook towards life and low self esteem.

How safe is the internet for our children??

The sexual victimization of children is overwhelming in magnitude yet largely unrecognized and underreported. Children are suffering from a hidden epidemic of child abuse and neglect.

Worldwide pornography revenue in 2006 was $97.06 billion. Of that, approximately $13 billion was in the United States (Internet Filter Review, 2006). Every second, $3,075.64 is being spent on pornography, 28,258 Internet viewers are viewing pornography, 372 Internet users are typing adult search terms into search engines, and every 39 minutes, a new pornographic video is made in the United States (Internet Filter Review, 2006). 79% of youth unwanted exposure to pornography occurs at home (Online Victimization of Youth: Five Years Later, 2006).

Child pornography is one of the fastest growing businesses online, and the content is becoming much worse. There are thousands of videos being shot each day to be uploaded on the internet. The latest trend is to shoot videos with Russian, Japanese and other south East Asian girls who may be in the age group of 9 to 12 yrs and label them as teen videos. There are many other sites such as punish. Com that show teenage girls having cruel and aggressive sexual intercourse with multiple adult partners as a punishment for some behaviour. Then there are amateur videos again shot with school going or college going children. Some of the most popular sites are daughterdestruction.com, fistinchen.com, singlemom.com, exposedwebcams.com, dapink.com, defloin.com (site showing only deflowering of young virgins and it must be noted that hundreds of such videos are being uploaded each day on the net). In 2008, Internet Watch Foundation found 1,536 individual child abuse domains. (Internet Watch Foundation. Annual Report, 2008). It is also rather interesting to notice that of all known child abuse domains, 58 percent are housed in the United States (Internet Watch Foundation. Annual Report, 2008). The fastest growing demand in commercial websites for child abuse is for images depicting the worst type of abuse, including penetrative sexual activity involving children, sadism or penetration by an animal.

CHAPTER 5

RELATIONSHIP BETWEEN THE BRAIN, ABUSE AND HANDWRITING

The human brain is the most remarkable organ that allows an individual to sense, perceive, store, process and act on external and internal information to carry out the three prime functions required for the survival of our species:

- To survive.
- To affiliate and mate.
- To protect and nurture the dependents.

In order to carry out these core responsibilities, thousands of inter-related functions have evolved in the human brain. The brain has evolved hierarchical structural organization.

Neuro-archaeology is a branch of neurobiology that studies the structural and functional organisation of the brain. It is a study to capture the impact of adverse events on the developing brain, suggesting that each experience leaves a "record" within the brain.

A healthy development of the brain takes place when the child experiences a variety of emotional, behavioural, cognitive and social experiences at key times (age of functional maturity) during development. Any disturbance which either "over develops" or "underdeveloped" the limbic and cortical areas will result in an imbalance, predisposing the child to aggressive and violent behaviour.

A child in an environment characterized by persisting trauma such as domestic violence, physical abuse, and community violence will develop an excessively active and reactive stress response system. The majority of stress response systems reside in the brain stem and mid brain and development of stress, even in the presence of positive emotional /cognitive experience, will result in a predisposition to act in an aggressive, impulsive behaviour.

Experiences of abuse alter a variety of brain areas and functions important in predisposition to violence. If the trauma is experienced while in uterus or in the perinatal period, it will result in symptoms of anxiety. If the trauma is experienced in the first few years of life, it can impact the middle brain resulting in impulsive and aggressive symptoms. Trauma during infancy and childhood impairs the sub cortical and limbic areas, resulting in a depressed or unattached individual in adulthood. Such experiences throughout childhood can impair the development of cognitive capabilities resulting in violent processing and problem-solving styles.

Introduction to graphology as a non-invasive Neuro-psychological method of assessment

Graphology is a term first coined in the 19th century by Jean Hippolyte Michon and used to describe a distinct human behavioural science. It includes everything that a human hand can create: drawings, paintings, sculptures, and handwriting. Our graphic gestures, whether spontaneous or deliberate, distinguish each one of us from one another. One can evaluate intelligence and attitudes, tendencies and motivations, emotions and the dynamics between the conscious and unconscious mind.

Handwriting is an extraordinarily complex brain activity. The elements involved here are the brain, the nerves carrying the instructions to the muscles, the muscle fibres that hold the pen and so on. It is the brain that decides what the written letters should look like, how the individual should hold the pen or pencil, how fast or slow an individual should write and the like. Any change, anywhere in this path alters the handwriting. No two people have the same brain anatomy, muscle-nerve relationship or mental images of alphabets. *Therefore, Graphology can be viewed as a prime parameter to assess neuro-muscular-psychological development of an individual.*

Handwriting is as unique as the fingerprints of human being. Handwriting is a combination of conscious and subconscious mind of an individual. It is a significant projective technique being used by individuals, therapists and businessman, alike. Handwriting analysis is a graphic science, which is documented with remarkable examples from all spheres of life. It reveals many insights into personality including childhood trauma, individual identity and performance potential. As a scientific tool, it is equipped with an intrinsic capacity to penetrate the depths of the human personality. This quality helps graphology to easily correlate with all those disciplines interested in human behaviour like psychology, psychoanalysis, criminology, sociology, anthropology, psychiatry and medicine.

Characteristics of graphology as an empirical tool for diagnostic enhancement

The prime aim of Graphology is to create awareness of self in the client. Graphology gives a complete, wholesome view of any individual. The emphasis is on present state of mind and the immediate awareness of emotion and action related to it. Complete view of dynamics of mental, emotional, physical and behavioural traits and the overall resulting personality is presented in depth by the science of Graphology. Graphology addresses non-verbal behaviour to explain defences, manipulative acts and current emotions of the subject. In graphology, the stress is on the inner experiences of the subject and their explanations.

The diagnosis is not viewed as detrimental, and does not place the graphologist in superior role. Graphology doesn't use persuasion, does not criticize the subject, and does not ask questions that are not relevant to the subject, at that point in time. Total and non-conditional acceptance of the subject is encouraged by this science. One of the most crucial facets of personality is decision making, which is explained well by Graphology.

The famous educator Maria Montessori knew 100 years ago that hand is central in developing the intellect. Brain research now validates her educational wisdom. The neglect of intensive penmanship training that was emphasized in olden days has taken its toll. Most of the developed countries that have "progressed" from the notebooks and blackboards to the mouse and keyboards and they too, are facing problems in the field of health and education. *It should be taken as a warning by the countries that still have their educational system strongly rooted in writing, yet want to ape the west by reducing the practice of writing hoping to "progress".*

Therefore graphology, which could appear 'obsolete' to some, as it is based on the primitive concept of manual work, right in the middle of 'the internet and high-tech age' on the contrary confirms its modernity, thanks to the scientific rigor and technical efficacy!

CHAPTER 6

GRAPHOLOGICAL PERSPECTIVE OF CHILD SEXUAL ABUSE

According to globally accepted anthropological findings, the anatomical evolution of human beings was completed some 50,000 years ago. Since then the human body and brain have remained essentially the same in structure and size. On the other hand, the conditions of life have changed profoundly during this period and continue to change at a rapid pace.

To adapt to these conditions, the human species used its faculties of consciousness, conceptual thought, and symbolic language to shift from genetic evolution to social evolution which takes place much faster and provides far more variety. The nature of consciousness is a fundamental existential question that has fascinated men and women throughout the ages and keeps re-emerging as a topic of intensive discussions among experts from various disciplines, including psychologists, physicists, philosophers, neuro-scientists, artists and representatives of mystical traditions.

Consciousness is basically the self-awareness which seems to manifest itself only in higher animals including human beings. The rest is a part of the collective subconscious and unconscious. As individuals, we participate in these collective mental patterns called subconscious and unconscious, are influenced by them, and involved deeply in them.

Coming to the graphological explanation for child sexual abuse, it is seen that all the actions are explained by one, single theory of the "mind-body connection". This theory describes the "oneness" of the universe and a link between all forms of existence. It is based on the theory of "collective subconscious" and further points out that no matter who thinks / generates the thought, it will be manifested into an action sometime, whenever that thought finds conducive environment to grow into an action, and it is not necessary that the originator of the thought will put it into action. It can manifest itself anywhere, anytime and by anyone. The theory of Vedanta is also based on the concept of collective subconscious and therefore is similar to the graphological perspective.

As Dr. Thomas has stated "We do not have solitary beings. Every creature is, in some sense, connected to and dependent on the rest." It is noticed that excessive aggression, competition, and destructive behaviour are predominant only in the human species and have to be dealt with in terms of cultural values rather than being explained scientifically as natural phenomena.

In human brain, each human function and organ is given a specific place. Hunger and sex share the same centre (somato-sensory cortex) in the brain. We consider the hunger to be the primary need of all living beings but we never recognized sexuality to be the same. The fact is that sex has many inter related aspects linked with it and not only the act of sexual intercourse. Just as we need to eat when we feel the hunger pangs, we need to be touched with affection, gentleness and love on a regular basis.

To touch to convey appropriate emotions is the first step towards being able to establish oneself sexually, in a sexual relationship. When the child is touched with love and affection from birth till the age of seven, the foundations of positive sexual orientation are being laid. It is a human need to feel connected and to be connected, emotionally as well as physically.

Though the act of touching is seen and felt by the child and is consciously aware of the fact, the message that her subconscious keeps getting; is that she is lovable, she deserves to be loved, that her body is good enough to be touched with affection and that there is nothing wrong in touching someone to convey your care and love at any given point in time. Just as availability of food would reassure one's mind of being able to satisfy the hunger, availability of another person to satisfy the need to be loved and touched lovingly would assure the mind.

It is extremely necessary to be touched with affection, as number of laboratory studies have proved over a period of time that when the infants are separated physically from the mother or the primary care giver and are denied caring and affectionate touch, they simply die. It's important to take notice of the fact here that the infants were provided with all the necessary food, clothing and shelter that we consider to be the "basic needs". The need to be touched lovingly has existed since the beginning of life on this planet earth and will cease to exist only with the last living organism.

According to Graphological theories, from birth to seven years of age is under the influence of the mother / mother figure / primary care giver. During this period of time the child is supposed to get maximum affection from the mother. It is not necessary to have a biological mother to give affection that the child requires but having an individual around to provide the child with the affectionate and gentle touch, words and the actions that the child can see and feel.

As discussed earlier, this is how the foundations for a positive and stable loving relationship with another adult get laid. Just like the type of food required by an infant is different in childhood and keeps changing its forms in terms of consistency, flavour, and quantity as the child develops into an adult, the type of touch also defers at different levels of development. In the beginning, it's in the form of hugs, kisses on cheeks, gentle pats on the back, stroking, cuddling and the like.

As the child enters the school age and is about to become a teenager, the child starts avoiding these kind of touches on her own. Again, with the transition from a teenager into a young adult, the same person longs to be touched in the similar fashion as in childhood. The difference comes in the form of sexual connotations given to the touch by the society now, and involvement of a member of opposite sex instead of her mother figure. Thus, the same child who has grown into an adult now wants to be cuddled, kissed on the lips, and wants the body felt gently and stroked affectionately by another person of opposite gender.

Those children, who have not received this kind of touch at the right time i.e. till the age of seven years by the right person, will not be able to reciprocate or even receive a loving touch in adulthood. They WILL NOT BE ABLE to appreciate loving kind of a touch and its requirement by all living beings. These people will not be able to respect any good touch. And therefore, these very same children will not be able to have normal and satisfactory sexual relationships as adults in later life.

Not only these children will become harsh with oneself, and their own body, but also, they will be unable to respect their own body or anybody else's body and will be very uncomfortable with the thought of getting sexual/ intimate with someone else.

They will always give messages to themselves (their subconscious mind) that are irrational in nature, which will include feeling unworthy of love, undeserving of love, inferior to others, not having a body that is perfect to be loved, and the like. They will discourage those who try to touch them lovingly.

Similarly, when the child is not able to see the exhibition of care and affection by the primary care giver or does not get to hear positive and loving words about her, she is not able to reciprocate by doing the same to another human being or even appreciate if someone does it to him/ her.

The researcher proposes that the act of child sexual abuse is a two way process, like all other human interactions. There exists a child who is craving for a loving touch, and there is this adult, who wants to touch, wants to "show" his feelings by touching someone. When these two individuals come together, the subconscious mind communicates the need to be touched and to touch, in a non-verbal fashion.

If and when the actual incidence of a child getting involved in a sexual act takes place, it is the discrepancy in the form of touch required by each of them that stand out. Whereas the child wants affection and gentleness in a touch, the adult wants a sexual connotation attached to each act of touching. It is precisely this discrepancy that is neither understood nor appreciated by the society and therefore, this act is always condemned by all.

But, the research shows that the abusers are very proficient in knowing and understanding the emotional needs of young children. When a child molester or paedophile finds the void in a child's life and fills it, the child does not find it to be wrong. There is evidence of the void being a physical need such as food, clothing or money and the young child knows that if he /she break the silence, the gifts will stop coming.

The emptiness is an emotional state. When the child is told by the abuser whatever she wants to hear, is told that she is special, she is loved, the child likes it and starts feeling important and lovable in the presence of the abuser. This is the reason why most of the children love their abusers, cannot see themselves as victims and do defend the perpetrator until the day, when they finally realize that the relationship is harmful; mostly, when the child is well into adulthood . . .This is why we hear so many adults who finally break the silence and tell the now "horrifying" events that took place many decades ago.

The following figures are an attempt to illustrate devastating effects of "simple", "normal" and "common" patterns of behavioural responses, of the primary caregivers(whether biological or otherwise) towards children. It is observed that at times, the adults are so immersed in their own self centred thoughts that they overlook the fact that children are just as sensitive as they themselves are. Not only that, in addition to being sensitive, the children are alert and impressionable too which most of the times, we, the adults are not.

Emotions are the cornerstones of our life; therefore, a particular event may have totally different meaning for two different individuals. The emotions always surround the root cause of all processes, which is the DESIRE.

It is the desire that connects. It connects the mind and matter, the thought and the resulting action. Desire generates the field of emotions. Desire is also universal. Each one of us carries a baggage of emotions, and expectations at subtle level as well as at experiential level.

This tri-factorial relationship between the desire, emotions and the experiences is intricately designed and interwoven. The emotions lead one to certain kind of experiences, just as some experiences give rise to particular emotions. This dynamic process keeps one engaged through stages of life, one goes on without realizing that it's nothing else but desire which is responsible for running this universe. We, the humans, are just a tiny part of the entire jig-saw puzzle of life; be it our own life or somebody else's.

FIGURE 1:

UNFULFILLED STROKE HUNGER AND PROGRESSION
TOWARDS POSSIBILITY OF GETTING ABUSED

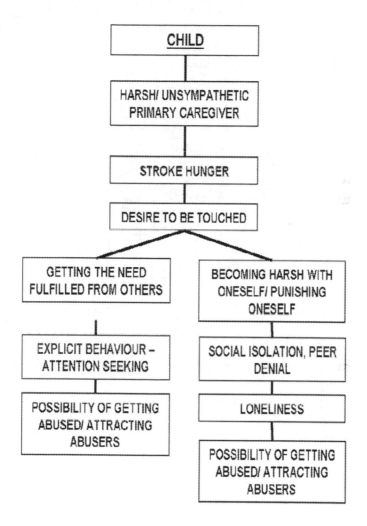

FIGURE 2:

UNFULFILLED VISUAL HUNGER AND PROGRESSION
TOWARDS POSSIBILITY OF GETTING ABUSED

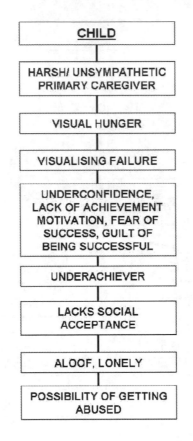

FIGURE 3:

UNFULFILLED AUDITORY HUNGER AND PROGRESSION TOWARDS POSSIBILITY OF GETTING ABUSED

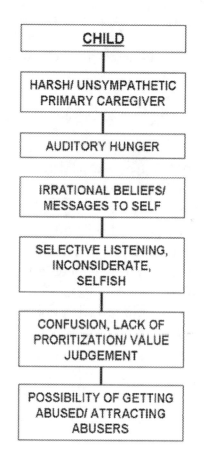

CHAPTER 7

RESEARCH DESIGN

This chapter describes in detail the framework and phases of the entire study.

Abstract

This particular study attempted to detect the presence of child sexual abuse and determine its severity in terms of mild, moderate, and severe degree. This was achieved by studying the representation of child sexual abuse in subject's hand writing in the form of grapho-indicators (graphological traits). The data, in the form of hand writing samples as well as clinical test for PTSD (CROPS) was obtained from a sample of 574 school-going children, from the cities of Secunderabad and Mumbai (India). Three different educational institutions and three different mediums of instruction, namely English, Hindi, and Marathi were chosen to reduce the class and religion bias. The subjects were in the age group of 11 to 17 years. The results showed that 301 children did not have any sexually abusive experiences and 273 children had experienced the same. The scores on clinical test were correlated with the degree of sexual abuse present in the handwriting. The handwritten samples were analyzed by a team of six practicing graphologists under the guidance of an expert senior graphologist. The findings of the study reflected the relationship between presence of sexual abuse in handwriting sample as a cause and development of certain negative personality traits, which were absent in samples without any sexual abuse. It also emphasized the correlation between the post-traumatic stress symptoms and presence of the grapho-indicators for the child sexual abuse. The results were investigated further statistically using percentages, t-tests, chi-square tests, ANOVA, and reliability analysis-scale (alpha), to determine, specific areas such as irrational beliefs, and factors such as defences, energy levels, having significant impact on the child's personality.

Broad objective: To detect child sexual abuse and determine its intensity in terms of mild, moderate, and severe from the handwriting of school going children.

The hypothesis of the study was as follows. The handwriting sample of the school going boys and girls gives clear indications (in the form of grapho-indicators) of sexual abuse and supplement or enhance the chances of early detection and/or prevention of child sexual abuse. The handwriting analysis clearly indicates personality traits and grapho-indicators associated, commonly found in the abused population and uncommon/absent in the non-abused population.

FIGURE 4: THE HYPOTHETICAL BLUEPRINT OF THE RESEARCH

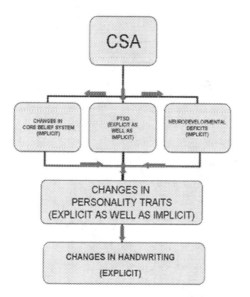

TABLE 1: OBJECTIVES OF THE STUDY

SPECIFIC OBJECTIVES	METHOD	PLAN OF ANALYSIS
1. To analyze the handwriting of the target population i.e.11 to 17 yrs. old school going boys and girls.	Collecting handwriting samples.	**Graphological analysis.**
2. To determine presence or absence of sexual abuse in the handwriting.	Analysis by grapho-experts.	**Graphological analysis.**
3. To ascertain intensity of sexual abuse in terms of mild, moderate and severe degree.	Analysis by grapho-experts.	**Graphological analysis.**
4. To correlate scores on CROPS for PTSD with graphological analysis.	Administration of CROPS psychological test.	**Statistical analysis.**
5. To determine personality building blocks of the entire target population.	Graphological analysis by experts.	**Graphological analysis.**
6. To note similarities and differences in personality characteristics, between sexually abused children and non-abused children.	Graphological analysis by experts.	**Statistical analysis.**
7. To detect grapho-indicators of negative personality traits present in handwriting of sexually abused children.	Graphological analysis by experts.	**Statistical analysis.**
8. To further identify irrational core beliefs in handwriting of sexually abused children.	**Graphological analysis by experts.**	**Statistical analysis.**

PHASES OF THE STUDY

PHASE I: public opinion

Keeping the need to have a different approach in mind and in order to assess the feasibility and relevance of the aim and objectives of this particular study, 100 ladies and men, above 18 years of age, from the city of Pune and the rest of India were randomly selected and contacted by the researcher. This was done in person (Pune) as well as on the Internet (other cities). The selected people were asked to write down their opinions on paper / in the e-mail, as a response to the following question "WHY DOES CHILD SEXUAL ABUSE TAKE PLACE?" The data was then collected, sorted out and presented in tabulated form (refer Table 4).

Outcome of Phase I

The outcome of Phase I (Table 2) indicated that the cross section of population has few misconceptions with regards to "why does child sexual abuse take place". It showed significant need for sexuality education for all. It also indicated there was an urgent need for an effective intervention, in order to reduce / prevent the prevalence of child sexual abuse in Indian society.

PHASE II: selection of sample, data collection and method

For this particular study, a mixed sample of 643 school going boys and girls were chosen from Secunderabad, and Mumbai (India). It was a deliberate selection of sample as it typically represented the population to be studied. Out of this, 574 samples were selected for the actual study. The rest were rejected on the grounds of illegibility or insufficient matter.

TABLE 2: OUTCOME OF PHASE 1

Sr.No	Opinion/Responses	%
1	People who are emotionally disturbed commit sexual abuse of children	66.40%
2	People, who have been sexually abused in their childhood, abuse other children when they grow up.	61.20%
3	Our culture expects people, especially men to repress their sexual feelings and therefore this takes place secretly.	58.38%
4	This is an indication of insecurity on the part of abuser. The abusers always try to attract attention of others.	57.14%
5	People who are deprived of love always indulge in such activities	47.50%
6	The children lack awareness regarding sex and issues. The adults take advantage of this fact for their own requirements related to sex.	42.88%
7	Men do this to bring about a variety in the sex life.	42.88%
8	Child sexual abuse takes place, when the parents have problems in their relationship (dysfunctional family).	38.60%
9	People who have had unhappy childhood, abuse children sexually.	33.33%
10	The youth and adults alike are exposed to the media including Internet, where projection of different kinds of abuse is rampant.	28.50%
11	Child sexual abuse happens only in villages due to lack of education	23.50%
12	Children are powerless and are unable to stop the abusers. Men do this for fun/ entertainment.	23.50%
13	People do this to take revenge on the child's parents.	23.50%
14	Men who are sexually dissatisfied with their wives abuse children	14.35%

TABLE 3: DESCRIPTION OF SAMPLE

Medium Of Instruction	Gender	City	Age In Yrs	Class	Type Of Educational Institute	Socio-Economic Background	Religions	Writing Ability
1. English	Boys Girls	Secunderabad	11 to 17	7th, 8th and 9th std.	School run by central Govt. of India	Upper class and upper middle class (annual income- Rs. 1,50,000/ onwards)	Hinduism, Muslim, Sikhism, Christianity	English and Hindi
2. Hindi and Marathi	Boys Girls	Mumbai	11 to 17	7th, 8th, and 9th std.	School run by Mumbai Municipal Corporation	Lower middle class and lower class. (annual income- Rs. 60,000/ onwards)	Same as above	Hindi and Marathi
3. Marathi	Boys Girls	Mumbai	11 to 17	8th and 9th std.	School run by Indian Govt. attached to a foster care centre	Slum dwellers, domestic workers, construction site workers and labourers (annual income- Rs. 12,000/ onwards)	Same as above	Marathi and Hindi

The data was collected in two steps. The first being handwriting samples, and the other was the administration of a clinical test for PTSD (CROPS).

Description of CROPS

Dr. Ricky Greenwald, Psy.D (NY) has developed this measure. This test covers the full range of children's post-traumatic symptoms as reported in the literature (Fleture, 1993), including those described as characteristic of PTSD in the DSM-IV (American psychiatric Association, 1994).

An identified trauma event is not required. This measure can be administered in any group or individual settings, in person or by mail or telephone. It requires a third grade reading level, but can be administered by interview to children as young as first grade. Each measure requires about five minutes to complete and one minute to score.

Thus, the crops is convenient and versatile, with potential utility in a variety of context, including treatment outcome research, and/or screening following a natural disaster or other critical incident, and screening for traumatic symptoms in clinical, medical and educational settings. The Crops provides a quick, convenient and effective way to screen children's post-traumatic symptoms, and to measure changes in symptoms over time.

PHASE III: Data analysis and report writing

1. **Quantitative analysis**: In order to test the hypothesis, statistical analysis was done using the SPSS (software program for social sciences, version 11.5). The data was analyzed with the help of t-test, percentages, Pearson's chi-square correlation, frequency distribution, likelihood ratio and the like.

2. **Qualitative analysis**: The graphological analysis was descriptively presented along with graphical representations. An expert, senior graphologist and his team of six practicing graphologists determined the severity of sexual abuse. The

presence of sexual abuse was detected with the help of grapho-indicators present in the handwriting of each child. The complete personality was analyzed in terms of the irrational beliefs, negative traits present due to sexual abuse, defences, fears, relationship with others, potential problem areas and the like.

The author hereby wishes to elaborate on the dynamics of the current social setting in India and its implications on this particular study.

The research design and methodology might seem incomplete to the Western counterparts, at a first glance. But unlike the Western developed settings, we, here in India face multitude of obstacles when it comes to studying child sexual abuse.

Why is conviction seldom achieved in child abuse cases in India?

Child rights activists say that we need to learn the speedy manner with which the trials are conducted and the way in which the media follows it up. The prime reason for perpetrators going scot-free is as follows:

1. The abuse goes unreported because almost always the crime is committed by someone close to the child. The family fears that its honours' will be sullied, and especially if a girl child has been raped or molested, they think she will never be able to get married if the story comes out into the open.

2. If it is reported, then the police show apathy towards the entire procedure.

3. An abused child has no one to advocate his case. Often, while the prosecution tries to be objective in building up its arguments, the defence hires the best legal brains and ends up winning.

4. Certain sympathy for fair-skinned offenders. People often feel that the foreigners are innocent philanthropists who are being blamed so that the urchins can extract money out of them, or they think the street children don't mind being used sexually for money.

5. Until recent times, there was no law or policy formed in India to deter people from committing this crime.

6. There are sexually abused girl, boys and grownups almost in all household. But almost all of them want to die with that pain in their heart. They do not feel safe yet to disclose their grief. Similarly, there are no perpetrators that we can get access to, especially for study purpose. Only a few are in police custody for raping someone and nobody is allowed any contact with such criminals.

So, here we are; wanting to fathom the impact of child sexual abuse, wanting to throw light on the everyday occurrences in the dark, wanting to give voice to the *silent screams* and wanting to put a stop to all that is taking place . . . but we have to cross the road without any support and ease. There seem to be a lot many obstacles in the way ahead; yet, the determination, courage and hope on the part of the researchers remain never-ending.

CHAPTER 8

THE RESULTS

The graphological analysis was divided into five areas, namely:

a) General personality characteristics of overall sample. These traits (21 in total) were grouped into seven behavioural components for the purpose of qualitative analysis as follows:

   a) Interaction with others.
   b) Potential problem areas.
   c) Drive, motivation and energy.
   d) Temperament, emotions and moods.
   e) Fears and defences.
   f) Positive traits.
   g) Self esteem.

b) Detecting presence of sexual abuse in handwriting. At this stage it was determined that 47.56% were sexually abused and that 52.43% children were not found to be sexually abused from the overall population (n=574). These results also happen to be in tune with the other studies conducted so far in India. Looking at the presence of sexual abuse in relation to gender, the boys and girls were seen to have almost similar presence in the category of mild abuse, whereas amongst the girls, there were more girls detected with the moderately abused category than the rest of the two. The percentages (56.7%) again showed that more boys were abused severely than the mild and moderate category.

This is a cause of concern for all those involved with children's safe and appropriate upbringing, because a vast majority of these incidents are going unnoticed, unreported and therefore untreated.

According to the literature reviewed, when sexually abused boys are not treated, the society later must deal with the resulting problems including higher crime rate, suicide, drug use and more sexual abuse. The studies have found that the suicide rate among sexually abused boys was one-and-a-half to 14 times higher and multiple substance abuse among boys who were molested was 12-40 times than those who were not molested (Dr. Homes, W. 2005).

c) Determining severity of sexual abuse in terms of mild, moderate, and severe degree. Important step was to determine the severity of sexual abuse. This was again done under the expert guidance of a senior graphologist, by his team of six practicing graphologists. The results showed that 165 children were in the mild category, 78 children in the moderate one and 30 children in the severe category.

1. The first category "mild" consisted of the vicarious abuse discussed already in the review of literature. It mainly consisted of the visual images of abuse that the children are constantly exposed to by the media, especially the television and the computer games. It includes all the violent actions, sounds and language that the children are exposed to in their environment, be it the home or the school or the peer group. It includes listening to the experiences of other members of the peer group, of abusive touches, of abusive looks, of abuse of comments that includes eve-teasing, and all the insecurity that is generated due to the above mentioned factors. Feeling victimized and vulnerable is considered to be the most commonly shared experience by the growing girls just before and soon after menarche. Such feelings create an unnecessary and avoidable stress in her mind and body, which is depicted in the handwriting.

2. The second category was" moderate" which included experiencing the actual abusive acts such as bottom pinching, the breasts or the genitals being touched in a crowded place by a stranger, passing of vulgar comments related to her body, lecherous and suggestive looks given by the strangers or the known people, her body being

felt/ touched unnecessarily by the elder male members of the family, cousins, or neighbours under the pretence of affection and being deliberately exposed to the sight of male genitals and the like. The same factors are applicable to the growing boys, who experience sexual touches by elder females in the family or in neighbourhood, lecherous or suggestive looks and stares at the genitals, feelings of shame and guilt for having an erection when in company of a beautiful, attractive elder women/ girl, comments being passed about his growing body by the ladies acquainted or not acquainted to him.

This first-hand experiences of abusive acts not only create related stress but also manifests itself in physiological processes like palpitations, increased alertness, feelings of shame and guilt, poor physical posture developed while attempting to hide one's growing body parts, feeling of anger towards oneself and towards the perpetrator at the same time trying to resume and continue normal relationship in case the perpetrator is related or well acquainted to the child. This again is a source of stress / imbalance and is shown very clearly through the handwriting of that particular child.

3. The third category regarding the severity of sexual abuse was" severe". This category included the abusive acts that are considered to be serious or criminal offences by the Indian Penal Code. Rape, digital penetration, oral or anal sex, being photographed or digitally recorded for the purpose of pornography, made to view pornographic films consisting of children having sexual intercourse or repeated touching over a long period of time are some of the examples of this category. Even serious threats of abuse or blackmailing can be included in the same.

These abusive acts can be performed by the adults known or unknown to the child, forcefully or under some pretext that the child cannot comprehend or by misguiding and bribing the child. These kinds of acts lead to the changes in hormonal and physiological processes and are manifested in the form of high blood pressure, consistent palpitations, fight or flight response, nightmares, insomnia, loss of appetite, and avoidant behaviour. The changes are accompanied by feelings of insecurity, shame and guilt as well as inferiority complex. These acts also give rise to feelings of being unworthy of good things in life or being undeserving oneself.

d) Detecting negative traits that could be present in handwriting due to sexual abuse. The review of literature for the research has indicated some of the traits that have been detected in this particular study. All of these studies were psychological studies. The graphological analysis has indicated several more intricate/subtle factors that are associated with the sexually abused like being harsh with others physically as well as mentally, having fear of success, being extremely sensitive about one's own physical appearance, lack of interest in daily activities and the like. This is one of the contributions of the study to the existent literature.

Table 4: **Negative traits present in the handwriting of sexually abused children.**

	NEGATIVE TRAIT	FREQ	%
1	Anger / aggression	N=240	87.59
2	Secrecy	N=235	85.76
3	Being harsh with oneself	N=218	79.56
4	Lack of confidence/ feeling of inferiority	N=194	70.80
5	Self deceit	N=191	69.70
6	Dishonesty	N=190	69.34
7	Being mentally harsh with others	N=186	67.88
8	Being physically harsh with others	N=177	64.59
9	Lack of concentration	N=175	63.86

10	Pessimistic outlook	N=166	**60.58**
11	Lack of interest in daily activities	N=162	**59.12**
12	Being extremely sensitive about physical image(own)	N=139	**50.72**
13	Social isolation	N=113	**41.24**
14	Getting violent/ destructive	N=163	**59.48**
15	Fear of success	N=119	**43.43**
16	**Sense of guilt**	**N=128**	**46.71**

e) Self organising traits found in the sexually abused children. Looking at the positive side of this unnerving issue of sexual abuse, the researcher tried to find out the positive traits that were present in the handwriting of the sexually abused children. This was considered to be very important mainly because these very positive traits would help the traumatized children/ survivors of sexual abuse to re-organize themselves, self-perpetuate and continue living in a non-disruptive and non-destructive manner. The traits were found to be as follows:

1) Creativity.
2) Curiosity.
3) Open mindedness.
4) Bravery.
5) Perseverance.
6) Integrity.
7) Sharing / caring.
8) Generosity.
9) Leadership qualities.
10) Forgiveness.
11) Appreciation of beauty.
12) Gratitude.
13) Optimism.
14) Sense of humour.

A very interesting question arising out of this information is that, are these traits an integral part of the personality of that particular child which are now helping him to reorganize or have these traits emerged in the form of defence mechanism after the experience of abuse took place ?

The variables studied were as follows:

a) Gender.
b) Age in years.
c) Medium of instruction.
d) Presence of sexual abuse in handwriting.

- The hypothesis was justified when the statistically significant results showed that the sexually abused children had higher levels of PTSD symptoms present, as compared to the sexually non abused children.
- The mean score for Indian children was higher (21) than the mean scores of German children (19).
- The original German test was adapted into two Indian languages namely, Hindi and Marathi by the researcher.
- It can be concluded that as the intensity of traumatic experiences increases, the child internalizes these experiences more and more. It is consistently evident throughout the results that as the intensity of the sexual abuse grow from mild to moderate and moderate to severe, the expression of symptoms decreases.

Following are the pen stroke formations that were identified in the handwriting sample of sexually abused children. The readers need to remember that Graphology is all about the formations on the paper and not about any particular language, alphabets or any other conventional images. Therefore, the attention requires being on identical formations anywhere in the writing of the child, without trying to decipher it or 'logicalize' it . . .

The grapho-indicators for sexual abuse
found in the handwriting samples

The only published study "Indicators of Sexual Abuse in handwriting" was done by Suzy Ward in 1996 (Journal of the American Society of Professional Graphologists, vol. IV). It was an attempt to replicate and expand upon the research done by M. Martin, who identified 34 atomistic variables in the handwriting of 2000+ sexually abused individuals.

The above mentioned study was chosen as a reference point, due to one advantage i.e. the sample was collected from 76 known survivors of child sexual abuse.

The researcher has found 41 characteristic traits out of which many happen to be identical to the ones found in Suzy Ward study. This finding has lent confidence not only to the researcher but also to the validity of graphological analysis, on the whole. It also brought about the universality of children's responses.

1) Retraced strokes.	22) Narrowness within words.
2) Flames in UZ.	23) Narrowness between words.
3) Flames in LZ.	24) Narrowness within letters.
4) Isolated letters.	25) Illegible signature.
5) Isolated words.	26) First name larger than the last name.
6) Narrow left margins.	27) Isolated ppi.
7) Leftward writing.	28) Rigid initial strokes
8) Pinched ovals.	29) Overly large ppi in lower case.
9) Interior loops in ovals.	30) Extremely left slant.
10) Figure of 8.	31) Rigidly straight slant.
11) Excessive UZ.	32) Inconsistent slant.
12) Non existent UZ.	33) Arrhythmic writing.
13) MZ varying in height.	34) Unnatural breaks between letters.
14) Excessive LZ.	35) Pseudo-connections / soldering.
15) LZ stopping below the baseline.	36) Excessive corrections.
16) Non existent right margin.	37) Short lateral strokes.
17) Unbalanced left margin.	38) After stem lateral strokes.
18) Increasing right margin.	39) High set I dots.
19) Poor tri-zonal balance.	40) Other variations of I dots.
20) Precise letter formation.	41) Heavy pressure.
21) Uneven pressure	

It is extremely difficult to identify sexual abuse through behavioural indicators. There are no clinical tests available today that can detect incidence of child sexual abuse from the input given by the subject, except for confession or confrontation. Also, the observable behaviour can be misleading for the therapist as there could be other reasons for similar / identical display of behaviour. There are several behavioural changes that take place as a part of growing up and could be either ignored or go unnoticed by the parents / caretakers, which could actually be due to presence of sexual abuse. These symptoms can also be caused due to other forms of abuse, namely, emotional abuse, physical abuse and neglect. At such times, it becomes extremely difficult for anyone to arrive at a conclusion that is precise and factual. Child sexual abuse is a very sensitive issue and has to be handled with a lot of caution and care.

When faced with such situations, where any kind of doubt exists, Graphology can come to the rescue of the therapist or the parents by pinpointing the cause for the display of behaviour in question. Handwriting is a sensitive indicator of brain function. Graphology has succeeded in segregating the subconscious from the conscious in such a subtle manner that the entire personality is presented in a logical, sequential flow with minute details. The past, the present and to some extent, the future possibilities of the writer are in front of the graphologist within a few minutes.

CHAPTER 9

CHILDREN AND SEXUALITY

W hile growing up, most children engage in sexual behaviours at some point in time. These behaviours could be normal yet confusing and concerning to parents. They sometimes could be disruptive or intrusive to others. With the help of a very large research database available now, the knowledge of age-appropriate sexual behaviours that can vary with situational or environmental factors is at hands. This helps the professional to distinguish between the normal behaviours from the deviations.

Sexual behaviours in children range from normal and developmentally appropriate to abusive and violent. Concerned parents often come to the paediatrician's clinic with questions about whether their child's sexual behaviour is normal, whether the behaviour indicates that the child has been sexually abused, and how to manage such behaviour. Though earlier studies have suggested a strong correlation between sexual abuse and sexual behaviour problems in children, more recent studies have broadened this perspective, by recognizing a number of additional stressors, family characteristics, and environmental factors that are associated with intrusive or frequent sexual behaviours.

Therefore, it is of utmost importance to first differentiate between the two behaviours and then, proceed with the intervention. Children with sexual behaviour problems require assessment and more specialized treatment approaches.

Sexual behaviours are commonly found in children. More than 50% of children do engage in some type of sexual behaviour before their 13th birthday. The *awareness level of parents* and their acceptance of sexual behaviour as a normal one, directs parents to the guidance clinics. It is seen that mothers who are more educated and who acknowledge that sexual behaviours in children can be normal tend to report more sexual behaviours in their children when compared with mothers with fewer years of education and less acceptance of these behaviours. Several additional factors modify the extent and nature of the child's sexual behaviour such as age of the child, developmental stage of the child, family environment, and parental behaviour and response to the child. Parents who are not comfortable with their child's gestures or behaviour tend to panic, get angry and humiliate the child. Some children may display sexual behaviours that are common and age-appropriate but that can become problematic and require intervention if behaviour is disruptive to others. It should be noted that normal sexual behaviours usually diminish /become less apparent with admonishment from the parents, and although such behaviours may result in feelings of embarrassment in the child, feelings of anger, fear, and anxiety are uncommon. Reassurance and guidance about normal sexual behaviours can satisfy the curiosity. A 3-year-old who begins to masturbate before falling asleep may simply have discovered a self-soothing technique, may have seen the genitals of a new sibling, or may be responding to the stress of a tiring day. Appropriate parental responses are key to managing such behaviours.

In a study of children aged 2 to 5 years without any history of abuse, common sexual behaviours reported by caregivers included touching their genitals at home and in public, showing their genitals to others, standing too close, and trying to look at nude people. These behaviours do not vary significantly when boys are compared with girls across all age groups, but they do diminish in both boys and girls after 5 years of age.

Children with sexual behaviour problems are more likely to have additional internalizing symptoms of depression, anxiety, withdrawal, and externalizing symptoms of aggression, delinquency, and hyperactivity. This association suggests that some sexual behaviour occur within a continuum of behavioural problems with multiple causes.

Another group of children may engage in a greater variety and frequency of sexual behaviours that may be disruptive to others but not necessarily abusive. These behaviours are often noted after a shift in care giving environments; examples include children placed in residential cares and children who attend day care.

Younger children are less aware of how their behaviour may be construed as sexual or inappropriate. Reactions of embarrassment and shame by others may be misinterpreted as positive responses, prompting the child to persist the sexual behaviour.

Factors affecting display of Sexual Behaviours

- Depending on the child's developmental level, changes in environment and situations may result in an increase in sexual behaviours. Preschool-aged children are naturally inquisitive and undergo periods of enhanced awareness of their environments. Recognition of physiological gender differences occurs during this time and contributes to inquisitive viewing and touching of other children's genitals. This curiosity-seeking behaviour tends to occur within the context of other similar, nonsexual explorations. The birth of a new sibling, suddenly viewing another child or adult in the bathroom, or seeing their mother breastfeed can trigger or amplify children's sexual behaviours. These behaviours tend to diminish if handled appropriately by the adults around.

- Sexual behaviour problems in children are significantly related to living in homes in which there are disruption because of poor health, criminal activity, or violence. The greater the number of life stresses—including parental battering, death, or illness requiring hospitalization; deaths of other family members; and child illness requiring hospitalization—the greater the number and frequency of sexual behaviours observed in children. Because child abuse and neglect are more common in homes characterized by violence and criminal activity, children with sexual behaviour problems who reside in such homes should be carefully assessed for abuse and neglect. Among children with a history of sexual abuse, 52% indicated that they had lived with an adult who indulged in battering during their childhood, and 58% of the child sexual offenders who were in-home males also battered their adult female partner. As many as 68% of children with sexual behaviour problems have witnessed intimate partner violence among their caregivers. Adult violence in the home is strongly linked to abuse, neglect, and sexual behaviour problems in children.

- Children who reside in homes wherein there is family nudity, co bathing, or less privacy when dressing, going to the bathroom, or bathing or in which sexual activities are occurring openly are more likely to openly engage in sexual behaviours. Similarly, children from homes with readily accessible pornographic materials or poor supervision of children's access to such materials may use age-inappropriate sexual language and be more prone to engage others in sexual play.

- In the absence of sex education at home and at school, various forms of media has been a primary source of information for many adolescents. This information is often inaccurate, age-inappropriate, and misleading. In addition, early exposure to sexual content in the media has been linked to earlier onset of sexual intercourse among adolescents.

- Children with developmental disabilities may have deficits in several areas that can affect their sexual knowledge and activity. Such children may encounter challenges with social skills, personal boundaries, impulse control, and understanding what is hurtful or uncomfortable to others, factors that contribute to an increased risk of sexual behaviour problems as well as sexual victimization. It is strongly recommended that while evaluating sexual behaviours in disabled children, the parents as well as clinicians should focus on developmental level rather than age when assessing whether behaviour is appropriate; an adolescent with the cognitive abilities of a 3-year-old may exhibit self-stimulatory behaviour that is consistent with his or her developmental level and inability to determine what behaviour is appropriate in public.

- Sexual abuse and physical abuse are both associated with sexual behaviour problems in children. Interestingly enough, the manifestation of sexual behaviour problems may not immediately follow sexually abusive experiences. On an average, sexually abused children display sexual behaviours of a variety and frequency that is 2 -3 times that of children who are not abused.

- Neglect has also been associated with sexual behaviours in children. In addition, indiscriminate affection-seeking and interpersonal boundary problems have been reported in these children. Such behaviours are often manifestations of attachment disorders seen in abused or neglected children.

Abnormal sexual behaviour in adults: Paraphilia

When is it that the sexual behaviour is considered deviant or abnormal? Abnormal sexual behaviours that are characterized by very strong sexual urges and erotic fantasies are termed as Paraphilias. These acts may involve inanimate objects, children, or partners who are non-consenting. Paraphilias are usually seen in males and these tendencies develop in teenage. Psychologists believe that such behaviour is seen in people who have problems with their psychosexual development.

According to the statistical approach, an abnormal sexual behaviour is one that is rare, or not practiced by many people. A sociologist might define a deviant sexual behavior as a sexual behaviour that violates the norms of the society. A psychological approach states that the three criteria for abnormality are discomfort, inefficiency and bizarreness.

The paraphilias have distressing and repetitive sexual urges/fantasies/behaviours. These occur over a significant period of time and interfere with their day to day functions or satisfactory sexual relationships with other adults. These urges impact their lives negatively yet they find themselves unable to control the same.

A few examples of such behaviour are exhibitionism, Fetishism, Sexual Sadism and Masochism, Frotteurism, Paedophilia, Voyeurism and Gender identity disorders.

Options available to manage abnormal sexual behaviour:

Medical Interventions are inspired by the notion that sexual variations are caused by biological factors. Various medical treatments for sexual variations have been tried over the last century. This upsurge was a part of the trend toward using anti-psychotic and antidepressant drugs to treat a variety of emotional disorders. The best results are obtained with men who are highly motivated to change their behaviour.

Cognitive Behavioural therapies include therapy to reduce inappropriate sexual arousal and enhance appropriate arousal. Behaviour therapy in the form of aversion therapy and covert sensitization has been used successfully to remodel the learned paraphiliac pattern.

Insight-oriented psychoanalytic psychotherapy has proved to be effective for the paraphilias. Modification of distorted thinking, challenging rationalisations that the person uses to justify the undesirable behaviour and helping the person identify and control or avoid triggers of the behaviour.

Skills training-Social skills training may include training on how to carry on a conversation, how to develop intimacy, how to be appropriately assertive and identifying irrational fears which are inhibiting the person. These programs may also include basic sex education. If a person needs to learn and practice sexual interaction skills, one approach would be to have him interact with a trained partner.

Dual sex therapy is a modified version of the 'Masters and Johnson' approach offers the best behavioural framework. This has two purposes: to provide a method for the gradual establishment of a satisfactory sexual relationship, and to assist in the precise identification of factors that are contributing to the couple's difficulties. In order to improve communication between the partners, specific guidelines are provided to enable them to express their sexual needs and fears, and to help each learn how best to provide the other with sexual stimulation. Psychotherapy session follows each new exercise period, and problems and satisfactions are discussed.

The readers hopefully got a glimpse of the consequences that faulty behavioural as well as communication patterns can turn into. One can observe herein that most of these deviant behaviours get established in childhood or teen years. Therefore, Training one to be a better equipped parent always adds on to the quality of parenting, prevention of deviations and the higher satisfaction levels in the long term.

CHAPTER 10

PARENT –CHILD RELATIONSHIP: THE FOUNDATION OF PSYCHOLOGICAL ADJUSTMENT

A new born child is totally dependent on the biological parents or primary care giver for the satisfaction of his / her needs. A child grows up in close physical proximity of this adult and during the process of growth and development, connects emotionally with the care taker as well. In fact, it is observed that the physical and emotional development go hand in hand and are interdependent most of the time across the life span. At the same time, their social and personal references remain dynamic. Consequently, the expression changes too.

The five senses that we human beings possess are a window to the outer world. A child uses her sense of smell, sound, taste, touch and vision to understand, interact and respond to the immediate environment and makes adjustments that are necessary to lead a satisfactory life. These senses also are a tool to express our emotions, feelings and thoughts and thus, connecting the inner world with the outer one! When there is a harmonious exchange and flow between these two worlds, the individual experiences satisfaction and is motivated to go on.

When a pre-schooler hugs, kisses or touches her mother / father in public, it is considered to be a positive display of affection and is encouraged socially too. But as soon as the children get into adolescence, they are not encouraged to touch any member of opposite gender or display their affection in any other way but verbally. In fact, the child hardly gets to see adults expressing their emotions to other adults or children in various ways. Thus the child is bound to feel restricted and limited in choices. All this is a part of our faulty socialisation, behavioural ways and means, that we proudly expose our children to . . . we completely disregard the fact that the very emotions and their expression that we miss in our lives, will be missing in our child's life as well because we are unable to give them different models to refer to.

So, as a result, we see that the moment a child enters the 'teens', and the menarche sets in, we start losing our sleep as parents. Our parents never trusted us, how can we trust our teenaged children?? We imagine them to be overly sexual beings. We imagine that they are going to break each and every rule of the society to which we proudly belong (conveniently forgetting the fact that we ourselves broke the same rules given by the same society as well!) . . . We imagine that the child is going to harm the hard earned family reputation, built over a long period of time . . . Unable to accept the fact that we wouldn't have to lose sleep over this, *ONLY IF, WE,* provide our children with socially approved ways that satisfy their needs while growing up . . . at every stage of growth and development.

In the USA, the school going children are pressurised by their peers to have friends of the opposite sex. If a child of 12-13 yrs of age, does not claim to have a 'boy" or a "girl" friend for oneself, then one has to face ridicule from the peer group. The underlined need here is to experience the same physical proximity, affection, care, that they did experienced as an infant, a toddler, a pre-schooler. This need to feel a warm, loving human touch gets combined with the curiosity to know the changing bodies of each other . . . *they get into kissing, cuddling, petting. This is nothing but a beautiful way to give each other well deserved attention and a loving touch.* The sexual connotation and urges are forced upon them at much earlier age than normal, by the unloving / unsupportive adults and the media. ONLY IF - we could understand this and modify our ways . . .

Many interesting experiments have been conducted in or out of the laboratories to understand the human needs and the effects of not satisfying them or vice versa.

Kibbutz, a community living and farming model that came up in Israel, out of their societal needs, has proved to be a valuable lesson learnt for the entire humanity. This came into existence after the industrial revolution and the War - I, when the women had to come out of the house to earn money to sustain themselves. That gave rise to the concept and movement of women's liberation across the world.

The children had to pay the price for gender equality . . .

In the Kibbutz, the children, 8-10 of them in one house (crèche), were looked after for five days a week, by the women who volunteered to be engaged in child rearing services. The children were sent to their family homes on the weekends when their parents had a free day. As these children grew up into adults, they were seen to display a whole range of mental and emotional disorders.

Every child has a right to be cared for, to be loved, to be paid attention to. One must appreciate the fact that the U.N. (United Nations) has taken a note to mention this in the child's rights list.

When the senses of the child remain ungratified, the consequences give rise to various faulty thinking patterns as well. It is important to mention here that although we focus on the fallout in the form of irrational thoughts, the process of building up these faulty patterns / pathways is led by the sympathetic nervous system in the body that gets activated when an individual experiences stress. The moment this particular system is turned on by the body, it puts the brain on irrational thinking mode. The reason? Survival without getting misled or confused by thoughts! As the danger ceases to exist, the parasympathetic nervous system gets activated and brings the body back to its normal, balanced state of functioning. But when the danger signal does not get switched off, then these stressful responses become integrated into one's personality and have long lasting effects on the personal, socio-emotional, and intellectual life of an individual.

TABLE 5: EMOTIONAL INTERACTIONS BETWEEN PRIMARY CAREGIVER AND CHILD

emotions felt and / or expressed by infant	examples of appropriate responses of caregiver	examples of inappropriate emotional and other responses of caregiver
Interest	Interest / curiosity, praise, encouragement	Disinterest, annoyance, anger, removal of source of interest
Joy and laughter	Joy, pride, laughter, enthusiasm in sharing	Indifference, annoyance, anger, threatening (shut up!)
Distress	Comforting verbally and physically	Ignoring, rejecting, indifference, mocking
Anger	Disapproval, disappointment, reassurance	Greater anger, submission, threat or violence
Fear	Comforting, reassuring, explaining, praising (the fear may well be justified and necessary)	Anger, irritation, mockery, isolating, violence, threatening

The effects of need-frustration in children have been well established by Psychological theories and experiments. When the personality as a whole, suffers frustration, then there are three responses in progression that are documented by global researchers. Firstly, the child displays responses by projecting her anger and resentment onto objects and persons in the external world. Secondly, as the socialisation process inhibits externally directed aggression, the child shows responses by directing aggression and punishment towards oneself and then feeling guilt and remorse for the same. Thirdly, the child displays responses, by attempting to repress the entire frustrating experience and learn to live harmoniously with both; the external world as well as with one self.

Only aspect that we researchers strongly reject is the fact that the child is not ready for sex, in any way. Sex is not a part of child's reality . . . her world . . . her dreams . . . or her needs.

This fact is of paramount importance in order to understand HOW we as parents need to modify our own behaviour to protect our children. This is important for those parents who like to think that the only three things that they need to provide their child are: Food, Shelter and Clothing. That is the reason why it is evident that the children who experience sexual abuse are affected by factors, other than the three mentioned above.

These other factors include low self esteem, lack of sexuality education, lack of care-giving by adults, parental divorce or separated parents, withdrawn or isolated behaviour, depression, sickness and financial challenges. It is therefore, crucial for the parents to focus on the traits that are appropriate for healthy development and adjustment. These traits include

1. **Independence:** It is seen that the parents don't allow the child to do carry out routine activities for their own convenience or due to insecurities. But when the child is encouraged to be independent in day to day life, it subsequently provides the child with a sense of mastery over the task at hand, confidence and positive self esteem. Thus, independence becomes one of the pillars of a healthy personality.

2. **Creativity**: It is interesting to find most of the parents ignoring this critical aspect of development during the foundation years of life. The prevailing education system too focuses more on the logic and less on creativity. But the research has enough data to propagate creativity as the other pillar of healthy development. When the child is supported in letting her creative ideas materialize or is appreciated for the same, it boosts optimism

that the scientists display . . . to keep on trying new ways to achieve your goal. This is another pillar of healthy development.

3. **Interpersonal intelligence**: This would be the third pillar of healthy development. The child is allowed to interact with others, encouraged to communicate verbally as well as non-verbally. The parents let the child look at situation from different perspectives, develop good understanding of assessing the one's own emotions, empathising with others', also pointing out at the motivations, desires and intentions of those around them. Another very important factor is being able to resolve conflicts in groups. One tip that could help release a lot of fear from child's mind is to make her identify "good", "nice", "helpful", "caring" individuals around her. This is mainly to make her see that she can relax knowing she has a no of positive people in her life. *That the abuse is not everywhere.* That she need not doubt or fear every other person and anticipate abuse.

4. **Attitude towards the concept of 'give and take'**: It is observed with great pain that the new age parents are discouraging their young ones to practice this aspect of social life, consequently hampering healthy development. Children from early years are refrained from sharing their toys with other children, and borrowing anything is out of question as it is directly associated with the buying power of the parents. So, in earlier days, many children would play with a couple of toys; not because there was a lack, but also because they enjoyed it, and learnt many critical social skills while sharing . . . Nowadays, one single child has a cupboard full of expensive toys that her parents have proudly bought, but none to share with. This practice is based on insecurity and is reflected later in child's inability to ASK FOR HELP FROM OTHERS AND OFFER HELP TO THOSE IN NEED. When the help seeking behavior does not become an integral part of the personality, then the stressful situations can turn into calamities and irrational thought process can become a road block to safety and health.

The easiest way to lay the foundation of healthy personality is to develop ***reward pathways*** in day to day life.

REWARD PATHWAYS

STIMULUS RESPONSE

MEMORY  PATHWAY

SATISFACTION

The reward pathways are created when the parents respond positively to child's actions / reactions; it creates feeling of satisfaction in child's mind and installs a pleasant memory in the brain. Neurons have paved a new, positive pathway for the child to walk upon the next time, when she is presented with similar opportunity. When repeated for a few times, the pathway becomes clearer and available to the child for a long period of time to come.

Following are some of the guidelines for the alert and concerned parents:

- It is important to know where the child spends time.
- It is vitally important to know with whom the child spends time.
- It is a positive step to invite the child's friends over and to interact with them regularly.
- The child needs to know of a safe place in case he / she feel unsafe during your absence, a place other than your own house.
- If any individual is giving a lot of attention or gifts to your child, it needs your attention and intervention.
- While appointing helpers / baby sitters, it is your responsibility to give priority to that person's maturity, experience and trustworthiness rather than your convenience in terms of less salary, less distance from home or anything else.
- It would be best to talk to children about particular situation or actions rather than particular people to stay away from. We researchers know by now that 80% abusers include close relatives, friends, or authoritative figures.
- The child needs to know parent's address and cell phone numbers by heart.

Dear Parents, please believe in your own child. It is very important because

1. *Though providing with basic needs, care and protection are universally accepted as parental duties, Helping child learn skills related to self and society and working together with the educational system to enhance overall personality, happen to be two other essential aspects of parenthood that we have to add to the list urgently.*
2. *Children never try to give you imaginary stories about sexual abuse. They lack appropriate vocabulary, and they need your utmost support and trust.*
3. *It is but natural for a parent to feel shocked and angry when such an incidence is disclosed by their child. At the same time, it is the reaction of the parents that will decide how the child handles this*

extremely stressful situation in his / her life. Parents need to remain calm and listen to the child.

4. *It is imperative to remember that there is no single symptom of child sexual abuse. There is a set of symptoms that all parents need to be aware of.*

5. *It is most important for parents to tell the child that they love their child despite such traumatic experience.*

CHAPTER 11

PARENT- CHILD INTERACTION

Universally, becoming a parent is considered to be a rather stressful experience. It is known to add a whole range of responsibilities to one's already existing task list after marriage! The process of becoming a parent starts at the moment pregnancy test shows positive colours . . . and goes on till the end of one's life. It is said that especially in the Asian cultures, the umbilical cord is never really cut! Emotionally, the child remains attached to the parents forever. Yet, interestingly enough, it is talking about sex and sexuality to an adolescent and answering child's questions about the same, seems to be the most difficult part of it. There are two aspects of this difficulty; the first that the parents, especially Indian, at any age are not trained to do this job and secondly, they keep going back to their own childhood for reference, without modifying the undesirable aspects or strengthening the positives. The first aspect can now be dealt effectively with the help of all the experts in the field, training people to handle parenthood efficiently; but the second one of referring to ones childhood is easier discussed than handled! When an individual refers to one's own growing up days and the episodes of unheard of conversations (??), unique and unpredictable past actions; the individual gets a sense of great relief for having grown out of those experiences and never have to stumble on the same path again. This sense of relief lasts only till the time one looks at the innocent face of one's child, curious comments and impeccable observation! One can't help but go back and remember how one's parents handled similar situations. No matter how advanced we like to think we are with regards to the taboos, the code of conduct (both, conscious and the subconscious), the restrictions – all do continue to exist.

This is where, otherwise confident and smart parents start losing their peace of mind, get confused, feel pressurised by information overload and sometimes, do become worried and scared. They feel like avoiding situations wherein they got to answer awkward queries. They want to reason that "this" aspect of adult life comes naturally to all human beings and that the children will learn by themselves, somehow. They want to rationalise that just like they encountered the entire process in their childhood, their kids will do the same. Most of the times, the effect is either dissipating a little bit of superficial information or totally blocking the interaction with the child. This is one of the ways that pushes the children, world over, to get exploited or abuse due to ignorance.

The subject of child sexual abuse is still a taboo in India. The subject is surrounded by silence, a very large percentage of people feel that this is largely a western problem and (in spite of reading frequent cases reported by media) do not acknowledge that child sexual abuse happens in India; if at all it happens, the responsibility is bestowed upon some mentally deranged person. Part of the reason, of course, lies in a traditionally conservative family values and community structure that does not like to talk about sex and sexuality at all. Parents avoid speaking to children about sexuality, as well as physical and emotional changes that take place during their growing years.

As a result, all forms of sexual abuse that a child faces do not get reported to anyone. The girl, whose mother has not spoken to her even about a basic issue like menstruation, is unable to tell her mother about the uncle or neighbour who has made sexual advances towards her. This child's silence encourages the abuser to continue the abuse and to press his advantage to subject the child to more and more severe forms of sexual abuse. Very often children do not even realize that they are being abused.

In a study on Women's Experiences of Incest and Childhood Sexual Abuse conducted by RAHI, some of the respondents have stated that till the questionnaire was administered to them they did not realize that they had been abused as children. They had buried the incident as a painful and shameful one, not to be ever told to anyone. Some deep seated fear has always moved Indian families to keep their girls and their 'virginity' safe and many kinds of social and cultural practices have been built around ensuring this. This shows that there is knowledge of the fact that a girl child is unsafe, although nobody talks about it. However this fear is only around girls and the safety net is generally not extended to boys. There is evidence from various surveys as well as other studies that boys are equally at risk.

A commonly observed fact is that parents feel awkward sharing the real, scientific information as it is, so they palm off something that sounds closely related to the subject, but mostly irrelevant, fantastic or misleading at times. To give an example, many mothers tell their daughter that all girls have two eggs in the stomach. When they crash into each other, the blood comes out of our body. So, you should behave like a good girl, you should not run about and jump and play with the boys now. But the daughter comes after a month and says, mom, I did exactly as you asked me to do, yet why did my eggs break and why am I bleeding . . . Do these parents have any answer to this question? NO.

This subject is an important part of our lives and sooner the parents accept this fact, the better they can communicate with their children. They have got to provide a child with scientific information based on anatomy and physiology and remove all misconceptions from child's mind. Parents can always take help of the books written by experts in the field to describe or explain. Though, today with information overload, it is really difficult to determine which source is more authentic than the other; a little effort in that direction will help in a big way. When parents sit down and talk to their child about his / her body, it creates a feeling of confidence, trust and bonding along with some amount of embarrassment, if this is being done for the first time. But the effort is worth your relationship with your child and if his / her physical safety is your primary concern. The child gets a feeling that my parents do understand what I am going through and brings the child closer to the parents. What else would the parent really want from their child?? Learning, how to dissipate this information is made easier for the benefit of all the parents who read this book . . .

We have to begin from the primary fact that all living beings reproduce. It is a sign of being alive! Be it insects, plants, birds, animals or humans . . . we all reproduce and therefore, we all have a special system called as "the reproductive system" in our body. Reproduction is a natural process just like eating, sleeping and playing! When reproduction takes place at the appropriate time, appropriate place and in an appropriate manner, it becomes a healthy and joyous process. There are certain rules that the Nature applies to different species and if we follow those rules, we procreate healthy beings. Just like the mosquitoes lay eggs every third day and trees bare fruits from 1-3 yrs, the human beings can reproduce after the girl starts with her menarche (anytime between 9-16 yrs.) and the boys become capable of producing semen of required quantity and quality (13-16 yrs).

When the parents read this factual information, they are convinced that it's not too difficult to talk about this!!

It does become difficult for a parent when one is bombarded with questions and one doesn't really know how to answer them in a way that the child understands easily. One does not know how to use the vocabulary that the child uses or to go to his / her level of understanding so that the information is received with clarity.

Questions such as, "Where did I come from, Mommy?" "Why does that aunty have such a big tummy?" "Where do the babies come from?" If we notice, these are nothing but only one question, worded differently by different children and that needs one single answer! But it is also amusing to find different parents giving different answers to it! Some of the varieties of answers are, "God gave you to us!" "Children come from the hospital" "Doctor Uncle sent you to us, dear!" "Your mom and I went to the market and brought you home" "Once we went to a park and saw you playing there. We thought you were very cute and so we decided to get you home!" so on and so forth!!

When such "far from fact" information is coupled with the vulgar and suggestive portrayal of sex and sexuality, doled out constantly by the audio-visual media, imagine the state of confusion and anxiety the children get into . . .

Most of the TV channels transmit information about sex and sexuality in the form of commercials, documentaries, serials, movies, news reports and songs. These programs are shown to handle issues like murder, rape, molestation, eve-teasing, prostitution, birth control devices, HIV/AIDS, sanitary napkins through suggestive words and expressions. The media probably has a noble aim of educating adults in the country, but the natural curiosity of the children gets stimulated (and satisfied too!) in the process. If a child who watches an advertisement in the normal course of TV viewing, and wants to ask questions about the same, how many of us really answer them satisfactorily?? The fallout of such a response is that the child tries to find out the answer through some other means. *The research studies show that many children fall into abuser's trap while going through this process of finding answers- by themselves . . .*

A three year old girl glances at her father taking a shower and calls out to her mother saying "mommy came fast and look at the small tail daddy has got!" How do you think the mother could respond to this? By giving her one tight rap and pulling her away from the bathroom, or looking at her with angry eyes or simply tell her that it is not a tail as she thinks but that boys and girls have different looking organs to urinate and all boys have their place of organ look like this when they grow up into men.

A five year old boy sees a packet of sanitary napkins his mother bought from the supermarket and asks her "are these your diapers, mother?" How could she react to this, you think?? "Stop bothering me" "that is none of your business" "you should not ask such questions" or "yes, are a kind of diaper. All mummies need to use these sometime because a little bit of blood comes out of mommy's body. It does not hurt mommy and it is ok with us. But we do use toilets to urinate and morning routines." Children are observed to be satisfied with such an answer most of the times. It is the fear of the unknown that the parents get hampered by.

Guidelines for parents

Psychologists, counsellors, police and teachers, world over, have created a database of the problems faced by the parents and children regarding sex and sexuality. Some of the outcomes of their research are shared here with the readers.

When the child is three year old, he / she need to be taught all the names of the organs of her body, irrespective of the gender. It does happen in most of the houses, that after "knees" they jump up to the "stomach" or vice versa! When one takes a look at the available charts of body parts in the market, they too have genitals missing!! If the child can identify a finger, a naval, a neck or a leg, she should just as well be able to identify her own vagina or penis, isn't it?? It is very important to remember not to label genitals with some funny, amusing or any type of code words. Playing a game of "doctor-doctor" can be of immense help to both, the child as well as the parent!

The best time to talk to your child about sexuality is WHENEVER THE CHILD ASKS! The child shows her readiness to receive an answer by asking a question. We, the adults, have to respond to their readiness appropriately without procrastinating further. The only care we have to take is to use vocabulary and terminology that is commensurate to the child's level of understanding and familiar vocabulary. Some enthusiastic parents have discussed the entire reproductive system and processes with the preschooler when asked "where did we come from?" least realising what the child meant by that question. After half an hour, the child said in a confused tone "A new girl in my class said they came from Hyderabad . . . Like that, where did we come from?"!!

The answer could be "your mom and I decided to have a baby of our own, who would live with us in the same house, go out with us and have fun and to whom we could give a lot of love and happiness. So, we came very close to each other, hugged each other and that's when you were made. Then, you started growing in the special bag in your mom's tummy and stayed there for nine months . . . When you were ready to come out, the doctor helped us get you out of mommy's tummy and bring you home!"

World over, it is seen that most 6 yrs. olds were satisfied with this answer . . .

There is a school of parents who strongly believe that there children need to be enlightened, groomed and made responsible by the school authorities and the teachers. It's high time that these parents accepted their own responsibility and faced it positively. They got to remember that the child goes to school only for a certain period of time and the rest, she spends at home. The experts feel that the child has to be made aware of her own body with appropriate terminology before she enters the school.

Another aspect to be remembered is that even though the schools impart this information, it is at a very formal, technical and generic level. It tells them about the human reproductive system, the organs and their respective functions. *It is the parent who could weave in the emotional, social and physical aspects of life together . . . only they could talk about their family values and the expected code of conduct . . .* Just think about a girl who studies the reproductive system at school and gets sexually abused by a male relative in the house . . . I chose to take this example as this happens to be the most common occurrence in the educated community, globally. How good is that bookish knowledge for her, if there is absence of a caring, trusting relationship with at least one of the parents? It is necessary to have a conducive environment in the family that is open to dialogue, encourages and supports communication between the parents and the child at every level.

There is another serious reason for which I strongly urge the parents reading this Silent Screams book to open the channels of communication with their child, not only about the academics or extracurricular activities but also about their personal issues. Most fathers show great discomfort when it comes to such issues and just push it on to the mother, expecting her to handle it all. The mothers, though communicative and more in touch with a child's needs may not be comfortable themselves. They may feel nervous for having to face this situation alone. Also, it is absolutely necessary for the parents to remember that it is not their children, but *themselves who have the sexual connotations linked with different actions or words in their mind.* The child does not always have it. Many a times, the adults fail to understand that difference between their thinking and their child's thinking. A lot of friction could be avoided just with this one realisation. **They could at such times, take**

help of the doctors, psychological counsellors, school counsellors or the books written by the academicians (authentic and established sources). At the same time, one needs to take care of the fact that the perspective of the content will be dependent on who the author is. If it is written by a physician, then the primary focus will be physiology/ anatomy whereas if the author is a religious person, the perspective will be moral and spiritual more than anything else.

Coming to the reason, it is a concern that the experts in the field are expressing about the direction in which our society is moving and the way it is happening.

Earlier in the fifty's, the girls entered menarche (beginning of monthly periods) about the age of 15-16 yrs., their daughters then entered at the age of 12-13 yrs. in the seventy's and their granddaughters are now entering the menarche at the age of 8-9 yrs. No matter how much we like to blame and point fingers at the household chemicals like phenyls, sprays, deodorants, plastic, pollution, treated foods, veggies and water, and last but not the least, television; the fact remains that this is a phenomenal cause of concern to us all.

The research has shown us that when a girl gets her periods before the age of 12 yrs., her likelihood of getting a breast or ovarian cancer increases by 50%. Such girls find the joys of childhood missing in their life. They feel burdened, embarrassed, avoid socialisation and get drawn to alcoholism, drugs and early sexual experiences and unwanted pregnancies leading to abortions . . . these girls show delays in socio-emotional development and this is what we need to think about.

In one major study conducted in India in 2005, it was seen that teenage girls consider abortion as a contraceptive measure without being aware of its consequences on their body and mind. They are going for abortions because they do not know of any other option. They are not aware of the real contraceptives and family planning devices. It shows that they were not taught by the parents to take their own self seriously and handle one's own body responsibly. Isn't this a major fallout of the parent's absence in children's lives and parent's failure to deliver their duty towards the child' safety, security and happiness??

There is another school of parents who say, "thank god I have sons and no daughters. I have no reason to worry." The attitudes and practises have changed a big deal ever since the homosexual relationships have been legally acknowledged in India. Young boys are accepting it as a normal way of life and their right to experiment . . . Having multiple sexual partners is just as devastating cause of worry for all of us. We have the youth in the range of 16 to 35 yrs. falling prey to HIV/AIDS. Though the awareness campaigns have had their impact in certain regions and particular populations, those infected are now experiencing the full blown disease. We are bound to see the effects in the coming 15-20m yrs. But till then, can we not do something to at least inform our own children about these life issues and choices they would have to make responsibly??

Just a reminder . . . while we guide, coax, lead and walk with our dear children towards a healthy and safe life style, we, as parents, too grow and become better individuals with increased self esteem !

CHAPTER 12

REAL CHILDREN, REAL LIVES!

Truth is really stranger than fiction!

This space is all about the real life! It may seem far away from the theoretical propositions and evaluations. But the fact remains that this is how the children around us are growing up . . . In conditions that seem so 'normal', 'safe' and deemed 'socially approved', but which are offering them fear, confusion, anger and shame. They are being labelled as the 'problem children' and taken from one therapist to the other whereas the problems are presented by the adults surrounding them who might need the therapy themselves. The training that counsellors and therapists get is at times inadequate to identify and treat such occurrences. Moreover, adults involved in such cases refuse to accept the consequences of their actions. They use money, power or influence to hush up the therapist. The moment they sense that the truth is about to be disclosed by the child, they terminate the therapy. They declare the therapist to be inefficient and express dissatisfaction with the therapists' professional attitude. They continue to blame the child for 'abnormal and weird' behavioural display and seek help to tame the child somehow. In many instances, the school counsellors and therapists have refused to handle cases of child sexual abuse due to these complications and avoid coming to an unbiased, unprejudiced and factual conclusion. They tend to say what the parents want to hear. And wrap the case up. Sometimes, the therapist takes an easier and convenient way out by identifying a particular behaviour / issue and work upon it rather than face the sexual abuse glaring back. This seems like a temporary solution and a kind of win-win situation where the therapist is satisfied for being a professional and helping the child cope up with an issue that was disturbing her day to day routine. The parents are relived as the main issue of sexual abuse is not touched upon and the can of worms is kept sealed tight. It is indeed too taxing, disturbing and emotionally draining for a therapist to deal with these cases.

And this is how we continue to perpetuate the laws of the adult world!

Till such time that the adults, whether they happen to be parents, teachers, relatives, neighbours, or strangers, take a moment to stop and reflect upon their own thoughts, feelings and consequent actions, the children will continue to get traumatised. They will remain frightened and angry. These same children will grow up to be the adults soon. They might have impressive educational qualifications, they might have enough material resources to make their lives luxurious, they might occupy positions of authority and power, but how will they feel inside? What kind of human beings will they be? Will they be loving, tolerant, nurturing as the adults are expected to be? Or will they be harsh, cruel, intolerant, emotionally numb and aggressive?

The author vehemently avoids labelling any living being. It is relevant to mention here that the author is well trained and aware of advantages as well as disadvantages of labelling. The readers won't find any conventional diagnosis/label to any of the case studies herein. This is a proof that we can help without categorising, without creating batches of psychotics, autistics or any other 'disordered' people. This is a practise to remain HUMANE. This is a flat refusal to prescribe harmful drugs, 80-85% of which have nil or insignificant curing ability (Dr. Deepak Chopra, M.D., 2012). It is a conscious decision as a professional dealing with individuals, to let them remain individuals . . .

(All cases have their names changed to protect identity)

1. Sonali, a nineteen year old girl, belongs to a well to do, educated family. She is smart, healthy and intelligent. She lost her father when in 7th grade. Hardworking as she was, managed to shine as one amongst the top rank holder's list in both the board exams.

Determined to become a medical practitioner, she didn't mind living in a hostel away from her town. The first year at college was good. Then, slowly things started to change. Sonali appeared restless, unfocussed. She would wake up in the nights screaming loudly, terribly frightened. She lost her interest in studies and refused to leave her room to attend the classes. Her roommate asked for a change of room and told everyone that Sonali was "possessed".

Sonali failed in the second year. She had to leave the college and came back home. She was treated by the psychiatrist for three years without much progress. Diagnosed with schizophrenia, she lived like an unanimated object, completely devoid of energy and enthusiasm. She did not even follow basic hygiene practices like brushing teeth or bathing for days together.

During this time, someone brought her last handwritten pages from the notebooks to the author. Graphological analysis showed presence of sexual abuse by a person elder and close to her. This was accompanied by a lot of confusion, fear, lack of confidence and feeling cheated by someone close. On further investigation and talks with her, she agreed with the analysis and disclosed that it was her elder brother who would visit her in the hostel on weekends and sexually abuse her. He threatened her every time she protested and slowly, she lost the confidence to stand up as **HE** was the one who should have been protecting her from others rather than exploiting her trust and body . . . She blamed herself for the situation and protected her brother because he was the breadwinner in the family after her father's death. She let herself drown in the depths of depression, hopelessness and fear.

Though Graphology helped Sonali deal with the root cause of her torment in a different way and slowly come out of her psychotic-like condition, she has totally lost out on her ambition of being a doctor. She now is taking a course in arts and managing to live an insignificant life.

2. Mohit, an eleven year old boy. Born to highly educated and rich parents, who were always very busy with their respective professions. Both of them had to travel out of town frequently on business.

So, they had employed a twenty something young man to keep Mohit company and look after him. The parents trusted him for his efficiency and rapport with their son.

It got them thinking when the teachers wrote notes, complaining that Mohit wouldn't write a word in the class, would distract other boys with constant talking and wasn't able to concentrate on activities. This was something new for the parents as Mohit had performed consistently above average so far in academics. They got worried, concerned and confused. Talking to their son did not yield any results. Somebody suggested handwriting analysis.

The results disclosed that Mohit was sexually abused that was limited to touching. Both the boys confessed and agreed with the analysis. In parent's absence, Mohit was asked to switch on the computer, go to the porn sites by the servant and watch it together. It was at times accompanied by touching Mohit's private parts. The feeling of being pressurised to do something that one does not want to do and the fear of the unknown distracted Mohit away from the studies. This went on for almost two years and caused the behavioural changes that were visible to others.

3. Richa is a girl studying for her undergraduate degree and stays in the hostel away from her parent's town. She is twenty year old. On the last day of her second year final exams, she came back to her parental home and complained of severe feeling of suffocation and difficulty in breathing. She also told them that she had been suffering from a very weird 'disease' that made it difficult for her to move around. She refused to get up from the bed thereafter and always complained of a 'tear drop sensation', as if there was a drop of tear rolling down her arms and legs. She was taken to the hospital where a battery of tests was performed. It included everything from a simple blood test to the MRI scan. All results were 'normal' and she was advised to go for a spinal cord surgery (that would not warranty any improvement anyway!).

On analysing her writing, it was found that she was in a relationship where somebody dominated her totally. Later, she revealed that she had a boyfriend there who forced her to get intimate with him. He coaxed her, goaded her, tempted her and threatened her too. She liked him but did not like what was happening between them. She wanted it to stop but did not know how to stop him.

To avoid going back to the hostel and getting into same situation, she subconsciously chose to get bed ridden and incapacitated in this way.

After three counselling sessions, she was able to get back to normal breathing and after 7 sessions, the tear drop sensation stopped completely. She decided to handle the situation herself and go back to the hostel. Later, she called off the relationship with her boyfriend and focussed on her studies.

4. James was brought for counselling for his suddenly rebellious, arrogant and insulting behaviour towards the family members. He is a twelve year old boy, member of an upper middle class family in Mumbai. His parents also shared their plan to send him to one of the best known residential schools along with a friend of his, about a year older than James.

His handwriting revealed that there was an element of sexual abuse present. It also showed a lot of anger, frustration and worry in his mind.

The same friend was abusing him sexually with a few other boys. He would show him magazines with erotic pictures and ridicule his expressions on viewing those pictures. Also they forced him to smoke cigarettes and now were asking James to steal money from his house to buy pornographic DVDs'.

With this information, the parents immediately cancelled the plan to send James away from home. Once that friend went away to the school (his parent's were informed about all this too), James coped up better and got back to his unthreatening days and nights.

5. Amit is a smart and intelligent twelve year old boy from Gujrat. An avid athlete in his school, he developed a strange condition in which

he was unable to close his palms to make a fist. His fingers would remain stiff and away from each other all the time. He could not do anything by himself since both the hands were rendered useless. After a while, he even stopped standing up or walking and started crawling like a baby, that too with somebody's support. Sometimes, he would cry out loudly as he could not close his eyelids and had to lay with his eyes stark open for hours. His parents were extremely worried and carried him from one specialist to the other, but did not get any satisfactory result. They were told not to expect any miracles and manage to live with the same condition throughout his life. Amit's mother had to take care of him like a year old child, carrying him to the toilet, feeding him meals and bathing him.

When he was brought to the clinic for analysis, it looked like a major challenge since he had not moved his fingers in months. On the first day, he only touched a pencil with his open palm! Next, there was an attempt to hold the pencil between two open fingers and scribble. After a couple of days, he was able to draw certain motifs like the sun, stars, trees and the like. Only after constant persuasion and practise, was Amit able to write a couple of lines and draw a picture.

Amit was under extreme stress. He was totally frightened. And he was sexually abused.

He told the author that his friend, a boy three years older to him from his neighbouring family, would ask Amit to touch his private parts even after expressing unwillingness. Both the families were very close to each other and Amit was threatened by his friend not to disclose this to anybody.

It took Amit two weeks to get back to his normal, active self! The hospital that had his file closed it forever stating it was a miracle indeed!

6. Ashish is a friendly, outgoing and academically superior boy, studying in class 7th. He is quite popular amongst his group of friends too. When it was observed by the family members that he changed his behavioural display which was drastically different from his usual self, they started wondering about it. He wasn't smiling any

more, wasn't interested in spending time with his family members anymore, and did not participate in any of the conversations unlike earlier days. He started sitting all by himself in his room, refusing to come out even to watch television or spend a lot of time with friends outside home. He also started arguing and picking up fights for negligible issues. The parents brought him in for counselling.

His father's elder brother, Ashish's uncle, who lived in the same house, would make him touch his private parts to achieve gratification. He showed Ashish pictures of children engaged in different sexual acts and asked him to do the same.

Given the kind of family dynamics, Ashish did not dare disclose his plight to anyone in the family but was most relived to share the same with the author upon prodding.

What could be the implication of such an experience? There is no hope for any change so long as the uncle status in the family is concerned. Ashish has to continue living in the same house till he becomes capable of making his own house. Will he be labelled as a "problem child" and made to undergo different therapies for behaviour modification? Will anybody in the family dare to stop the uncle from engaging in such an act? What kind of feelings will he have for the elders when he grows up into a man? What kind of feelings will he have associated with sexual acts and how will that affect his relationship with his wife in turn, if he decides to get married to a girl? Will he choose to become a gay?? Will this important aspect of his personality influence his career and the kind of success he expects to get in his life, as per his family and societal norms?

7. Sanjay is a nineteen year old youth, recruited recently in the Govt. services. He has been working with the machinery and was an average performer. Has a couple of friends in this new place of posting. One day, he is found crying in a corner of his workplace. He refuses to talk to anyone, just crying profusely all along. He is immediately sent to the hospital for investigations. His friends

disclose that for the last 5-6 days he was restless, unable to sleep, had lost his appetite and wasn't answering their questions.

His physical examination showed that the parameters were not under the normal range. His heart was beating at a very high pace than it should and he was numb, as if in a shock. He was totally uncooperative and continued not to respond to anyone. So, he was kept under observation for thirty hrs and on medication. The author was called in and after talking to him for more than a couple of hrs, he nodded positive to scribble on a paper.

The analysis revealed that he was under a lot of stress for last few years. His anxiety levels were very high and he was constantly worried about being physically treated with harshness and force. Only after a couple of days of developing rapport and enough trust, he chose to speak a few sentences about his older brother. His brother forced Sanjay to indulge in intimate sexual acts with him back home. Sanjay was scared to share this with anyone for the fear of being not believed. So, instead of studying further, he took up a job that required him to be away from his hometown and was getting a little comfortable with his life. That's when he lost his father and now, the brother became the head of the family. To his shock, the brother started asking him to leave the job and join him in the family business. This put Sanjay back in tremendous fear and anxiety about the future unknown. Such thoughts filled him up completely, rendering him unable to go through the day to day routine like his friends described.

It took a whole lot of convincing and assurances for Sanjay to slowly get back to his duty. He spent almost a month in the hospital recuperating. All he did there was to eat, sleep and draw a lot of drawings of his choice. He was asked to communicate only with his mother and letters sent by his brother were discarded by his friends without being opened, with his consent.

Though these measures might seem superficial and temporary, they are enough for a troubled and anxious individual to get a breather. it created a gap, a stopgap arrangement for him to gather himself back again to the feelings of being supported by others, of being safe, of being secure-physically as well as mentally and the confidence of being able to lead his life like any other young man of his age.

8. Jaya was brought for counselling when she suddenly started becoming very destructive, violent at home. She would scream, shout, and abuse anyone in sight. At the same time, she refused to be alone even for a moment during the day or night. She was seventeen and had never been scared of the dark ever before. Her studies were totally neglected and she suffered from severe acidity. She lost her appetite and interest in food on the whole. The parents were intrigued, confused. They thought it was an effect of hoodoo/ black magic.

Her notebooks were taken for analyses as she refused to co operate with the author for any other therapy or modality. It showed she had had abusive experiences in adolescence by a person known to the family. After sharing it with her parents, the father promised her that he will look into the matter and resolve it. But over the years, he did just nothing about it. Though the incidence of sexual abuse did not recur, the feelings of frustration, being cheated by the father and not being protected by the father whom she trusted filled her mind completely. The behavioural display was just a fallout of all these feelings, bottled up inside for so long.

This is a classic case where the child is living in a SUPPOSEDLY safe environment with most of the criteria for child rights being fulfilled. Her experiences have taught her not to trust anyone close to her anymore. How will this lesson influence her life a few years hence? What will she do with all the anger and frustration that would keep up coming back each time she remembered those moments filled with pain and shame and her father's promise??

Jaya was one of the few fortunate ones to have reached the counsellor's office. What about all those girls who go through similar events and live the rest of their lives like a living dead??

9. Sam refused to go to school and threw tantrums when his parents asked him to go. He is a twelve year boy growing up without any obvious problems so far. He even stopped going out of the house for any reason. He refused to meet people, didn't go to church, and spoke very little.

His handwriting analyses disclosed sexual abuse.

Sam was very fond of his teacher. The teacher decided to take advantage of this fact and started calling the child for extra assignments or voluntary work alone to the school. This is when he made Sam do inappropriate things with his body and did the same to Sam. Sam could neither fight back nor stop it in any other way. The person, whom he admired and respected, gave him discomfort in body and mind. How could he trust any teacher any time in his life? His mind became full of doubt t and suspicion. He felt guilty for his new belief that "it's better to cheat others, before they do so to us". He was frightened to think about his future. He started to avoid taking decision, taking any kind of risks. A friendly and playful boy started to turn into an introvert, fearful all the time.

10. komal is 8 years old. Her teacher (male) makes her touch his private parts. At home, she was beaten up by her mother for minor or no faults of hers and was scolded, threatened and punished severely often. She was told that children of her age have no sense of right or wrong and have to be punished for doing wrong things. She believed her teacher punished her too. She held herself responsible for adult's behaviour.

Komal was brought to the author for her obesity, and inability to control eating.

It is an extremely important part of the Indian culture to treat food like God. We respect food for the energy it gives us and respect the farmer for producing it for us all. Practises like ANNA-DAAN (giving away food to the needy), praying at mealtime and not wasting even a morsel, occupy prime slot in our social code of conduct. According to the theory of Graphology, food is a form of love offered to the children of the family to nourish and help them grow into healthy individuals. Withholding food or refusing to serve food to a child is an act of depriving her of love, care and affection that she has a right to.

Komal felt deprived. She didn't know how to handle this feeling. She wanted to feel safe, cared for and loved, like any other child. Food became the source of love for her. She grew insatiable by the day. She could never have enough. She tried to distract herself from the feelings of being unwanted by eating every time she felt low.

11. Kalpana is a 36 year old house wife. Always very shy and non expressive to the outsiders, she felt like a real volcano herself. she managed to pull each day with a lot of mental effort that others could hardly notice. But, in the last few months, she became a little more vocal than usual and thus, her friends could feel the negativity piled up in her mind through her words.

When her friends planned for a picnic next month, she said "I shall join you all if I am still alive." She told them that she was fed up of living anymore and wanted to end it all herself. Her friends took her seriously when they realised that she had been sharing similar thoughts with many of them, at different times. She was taken to the author for counselling for suicidal tendencies.

As a child, kalpana was abused by her father. He would touch her growing body inappropriately, combined with other gestures of fatherly affection.

Kalpana grew up to doubt every male's intention. She considered every male as a potential molester and was suspicious of her husband, too. She always feared that her husband had extra- marital affairs and would describe imaginary yet very logical sounding tales of how other men around her were trying to seduce her at any given point in time. The information she shared with others would be very convincing and easy to believe, but the fact was that it was but a piece of her troubled mindset and fertile imagination.

In clinical terms, she would be diagnosed with psychosis, probably with schizophrenia, delusional disorder (Erotomania) or bipolar mania and treated with medicines.

Her hatred for the opposite sex was so obvious through her aggressive, spiteful thoughts, abusive words mentioning revenge, various fears, tremendous anger and constant effort to keep her husband and growing son under tension of some kind or the other.

Kalpana took over a couple of months to relax, open up and introspect. Slowly, she could put the picture into perspective and came to terms with reality.

12. Ella is a 10 year old girl, studying in class 5th. She goes to a very well reputed international school that her affluent parents take pride to mention about.

She was sent to the school counsellor by the principal for repeatedly drawing one naked woman surrounded by 3-4 naked men. The class teacher was very upset and wanted Ella to stop drawing such dirty pictures in school. She also demanded that Ella should not be allowed to attend the school as her behaviour would have bad influence on other children and they might also start drawing such dirty pictures. The author was requested to analyse drawings and handwriting.

The drawings and writing showed tremendous anger towards father. The feeling of being cheated by an elder who she felt close to, were also evident along with fear of the future. She suffered from severe constipation and belching frequently. She complained of extreme pain in both the legs and feet too.

Ella's mother used to work at a BPO and recently had started doing the night shifts thinking Ella was old enough to sleep on her own. The father was a bank manager and would be home in the evening. Ella's nightmare began when her father started to invite his friends over for drinks in his wife's absence. After a few days, they started calling her to their room, asked her to remove cloths and stand in front of them, while they would gratify themselves in front of her. They all used to be heavily drunk yet nobody ever touched her body. They sent her back to her room once they were through with it. Later, they started getting gifts like chocolates and stuffed toys for Ella.

She was numb with fear. She neither knew what exactly was happening nor could imagine what would happen next? She could not get sound sleep with the constant fear that they might call her back to strip again. Then, in the morning she found herself devoid of any energy to go to school and study. She started missing school on many excuses. Her mother would come back tired in the morning and rest the whole day, to leave the house again in the evening. She would force Ella to go to school so that she could sleep without any disturbance. There was hardly any interaction between both the parents.

Who are the individuals that need counselling or therapy here?? Ella, for expressing her innermost feelings through drawings and alerting adults around her? Or the teacher, who instead of responding appropriately by trying to understand the situation, reacts unprofessionally with all her individual biases? Could it be the parents, who got so busy in their work that the child and her welfare was nowhere on their priority list? Or could it be the friends of the father, who indulged in such an act, without any compassion, gentleness and protection they ought to offer to their friend's daughter??

13. This is Savee. She is intelligent, highly educated, determined, and ambitious. A mother of two boys got divorced after 15 years of marriage. While married, she would invariably feel attracted to men much younger than herself. Off course, she would describe it as another man falling madly in love with her and desiring her. Savee married a guy almost twenty years younger to her after the divorce.

Savee treats her boys as well as her new husband with tremendous harshness and aggression. She is very calculative, pretentious and argumentative most of the times.

She grew up being one of the five sisters to the parents who were very religious, strict and orthodox. Threatening and scolding were the regular pattern of communication with the girls for both parents. Any minor or otherwise negligible act would invite the strictest of the punishments.

One such was to get the girl completely naked and make her stand facing the wall for a long period of time. This particular punishment continued to exist till the girls past ten yrs of age.

This severe encroachment on her right to self respect and being protected instead of being humiliated, left damaging influences on her developing personality. Savee lost her trust in elders and their ability to protect her. She learnt that she had to look after herself, take care of herself, and protect herself. To be able to do all this, she had to become aggressive, dominating, intrusive and pushy. She developed a terrible grudge against men and that was displayed through every action of hers. She always looks forward to getting close to a man enough to know his weakness and then to stab him point-blank with her blunt words and hurtful actions.

No matter how intelligent, talented or educated she is, Savee is labelled as a horrible woman best avoided at all times . . . but is she alone responsible for creating this reputation? Would she have developed another kind of personality had she had experiences that did not include humiliation, shame and guilt for being a woman, breach of trust, harshness and lack of respect?? There is seemingly no sexual abuse taking place anywhere in this particular case, but in essence, the childhood can be referred to as "abusive"; with a presence of physical as well as emotional abuse.

14. Sunita too is a clever, independent, knowledgeable, cultured and multi talented lady. She is one of the most popular professors in her college. She is married to a handsome, well established gynaecologist in her town and has one charming little son. The picture looks just perfect to any third person!

The moment her son was born, she refused to get physically intimate with her husband any more. Thinking she was suffering from post partum depression, he was sympathetic and affectionate towards her. They were very friendly with each other. They tried to understand and express love to their respective partners. She was lucky to have a mature and humane husband. He waited for almost 6 long years for her to give her consent and regain sexual relationship but to his dismay, she continued to refrain from the same. He was confused, curious and concerned; all at the same time. Occasionally, when he tried to open the discussion on this topic, she shared her thoughts of probably being a lesbian with him, although she wasn't sure about it ever. It was her effort to arrive at a logical, rational conclusion about not experiencing sexual desire.

Upon analysing her writing, it came to forth that she had had abusive experiences in her childhood. She convinced herself that she had forgotten them without realising that we can never ever forget anything in life! The only choice we have is actually to place them into two compartments, namely, conscious and subconscious!

Sunita was an only daughter of a successful, busy doctor mother and a rich, busy businessman. Both were engaged in their routines day and night and so, had a middle aged man employed as a domestic help. This man would look after Sunita in the absence of her parents. Along with taking care of her, he tried to discipline her in his own way. It is very interesting to observe that though anybody is capable of breaking, spilling, tearing or losing household things, it is always the children who are punished for the same! Adults always seem to forgive themselves for such actions! But the children take adults around rather seriously and comply with their regulations.

For such trivial matters, he would scold her saying," did you do it again? How clumsy of you, little girl? Now you deserve to be punished, don't you? Common, take off your clothes . . ." She would obey him and then, he would touch her inappropraitely.

For little Sunita, the concept of elders punishing children for committing mistakes was deeply ingrained. Just like her parents scolded her and the teachers threatened or hit her, the servant fondled her. To her, it was normal yet undesirable. It invoked feelings of shame, guilt and powerlessness in her mind.

It went beyond her tolerance when her husband, whom she loved very much, did the same thing to her. What was she being punished for, now? She just did not want it. She knew they both wanted a child and so somehow, went through the process till she conceived which was immediately after marriage.

Who is responsible for such distortions in a seemingly normal life?

15. Thirteen year old Dimple is the only daughter of a very well to do couple. She lives in a posh locality and studies in one of the best international schools in the town. She travels by the school bus every day.

The teacher sent letters stating Dimple's attendance was very poor and she may not be allowed to appear for the final exams due to the same. The parents were shocked but the girl would not respond. She said all was well and there was nothing to worry about. But the parents decided to take help of a detective agency to find out what was going on. They found out that she was really irregular at school. She would sometimes come in late or leave early but left and reached home on scheduled time. She was found to visit the family doctor's clinic that was very close to her school, frequently.

Intrigued, they contacted the doctor but he flatly refused that she was visiting him. The doctor's and Dimple's writing were analysed.

The doctor, who was in his forties, was found to have frustrated sexual desires which he chose not to fulfil. The girl was in a stage of development that made her curious to know all about sexual activities. He would make her sit in his room and play pornographic films. They would watch it together. He derived pleasure out of watching her face blush, her awkwardness, her embarrassment, her expressions of amusement and disgust. He never touched her. She attracted a lot of attention and envy of her friends with whom she would share what she saw!

16. Rachana is a thirty three year old architect and a mother of a lovely eight year old daughter. Lives in a beautiful town with her loving and affluent husband. She repeatedly complained of feeling suffocated, inability to breath, running nose and irregular pulse. She consulted various experts for the same but could not get treated

satisfactorily. All reports were clear. Yet the symptoms continued to exist. On top of this, she suffered due to the side effects of the medical treatment she underwent. Therefore, she wanted to get rid of the physical ailments desperately but through some non-invasive modality. Somebody suggested graphology to her and she consulted the author.

It was found that she would spend most of her time day dreaming of romantic encounters but was unable to put it into action. She thought about sexual activity all the time but did not actually indulge in them. She also had a lot of guilt in her mind. There was severe stress in her writing and a whole lot of self deceit combined with frustrated physical activity.

She broke down on sharing this with her. It was her relationship with a man before she got married. She was emotionally attached to that man even now and felt guilty for the same. She could never get close or attached to the man she married under certain circumstances, though he was a good husband. On one hand, she wanted to just leave everything and go to her lover, on the other, she reminded herself of the duties she had to perform as a wife and a mother. She had a very strong feeling that the time was running out of her hands and that she will never be able to get what she wanted. The uncertainty, confusion, contrasting emotions coexisting in her mind- created tremendous stress for her. Under the pretext of her work, she travelled to meet her lover and the dilemma perpetuated . . .

This example does not talk about sexual abuse but about the efficacy of handwriting analyses as a detection technique. It is totally non invasive, nonintrusive in nature and brings out the entire picture as it is. The individual does not have to answer any embarrassing questions or go through the trauma mentally again. It is subjective as well as totally objective in describing certain aspects of personality.

17. Mayank was a fifth grader who was brought in for counselling by his parents for not studying, being defiant, and sometimes expressing anger by throwing things around in the house. This

time he threw something hard on the TV. It broke into pieces. His poor performance at school got them worried too.

The handwriting analyses showed the child was disturbed, confused and angry. There was stress in his writing. But interestingly, there was not a single indication of any experience that would result in such display of behaviour. The source of stress was both the parents though, for sure.

The parents were interviewed. They confessed to fighting in the house often on the issues like father giving insufficient money to the mother to run the house and his long, unexplained absences out of town. Somehow, though these reasons could justify child's behaviour, the author proceeded to analyse their writings.

The results were shocking. Mayank's father had his nervous system badly affected. And he indulged in sexual activities with multiple partners out of marriage often.

On sharing this information, the father confessed ((in the absence of his wife) that he did spend a lot of money on prostitutes earlier and got infected with HIV. Then, he travelled to another town to get treated for which again he had to spend a lot of money. As a result, he always gave less money than required to his wife and the family suffered. The child witnessed all the fights, became angry and confused. The father felt scared, guilty and feared that he would pass on the infection to his wife one day. But, he didn't know what to do in such a situation.

All the cases mentioned here have certain aspects in common.

It was observed that no matter what, the children were labelled as 'difficult' children, were perceived to be undisciplined, lazy, or pretentious, and brought to the therapist to be counselled to be a 'good boy' or a 'good girl'.

It is noteworthy to mention here that most of the adults dealing with the child saw through the symptoms displayed by these children that clearly pointed out high stress levels. Do adults really like to believe that children don't experience any kind of stress other than exam related pressures??

It is a well researched fact that stress envelopes the entire personality to a great extent. Long term stress due to social and psychological life situations can be detrimental to overall health of the child. The human body is well designed to cope with short term stressors but when it continues for a long period of time, is compromises the hypothalamic-pituitary-adrenal axis. Stress also has been found to affect the cardiovascular, immune and serotonin systems.

An understanding of ecological factors is of utmost importance when it comes to community health. Maslow (1943) believed that humans strive to rise through a hierarchy of needs like physiological, safety, psychological, social and self- actualisation. According to this theory, human do not progress to the next levels until the basic needs are satisfied. We need health promotion systems to help people regain their psychological equilibrium. We need programs designed in such a way that people spend less time on the lower levels of needs and progress towards the higher levels. The kind of programs we have in India right now either focus on superficial symptoms or are not executed appropriately to achieve the aim. Our society is struggling with serious issues like domestic violence and child sexual abuse on such a large scale, a 'no-smoking' campaign or 'academic programs without life skills' make little sense. *It is high time that we stopped looking at the coping mechanisms as the main issue to be dealt with . . . Let us begin by facing the reality, let us begin by listening to the silent screams . . .*

CHAPTER 13

TO ALL MY GUARDIAN ANGELS . . .

Each one of us has a story to tell . . . a story of how we lived our life here . . .! I wanted to write an autobiography in my early twenties, because I had already seen so much, learnt so much, experienced so much and assimilated so much! I secretly wished that I was done and over with all the bitter, painful, traumatic experiences and looked forward to a life full of peace and happiness.

This is the story of all those who were with me whenever I was in pain . . . This is the story of all my guardian angels. This is the story of how they helped me go on, without giving up on life. This is the story of all those whom I love dearly.

They say that each one of us has two angels to protect us during our life on earth. I am one of the luckiest people to have had so many of them, one after the other. Different ones for different situations, for different ages, for different geographical locations . . . But, I was never left alone for sure.

Life is all about perception. You change your perception, you change your life! All the while I would fret and frown that I was all alone in this world, missing out on recognising the angels who constantly kept me company. I did appreciate their presence in my life at that time and was grateful to them, but never perceived them to be my angels! Today, I do so, with whole hearted gratitude and love.

Till the time we do not accept the fact that the relationships are for us to become aware and conscious of ourselves, of our progress, and not necessarily a source of happiness, we keep struggling with them. The moment we realise and accept that they are our teachers, teaching us tough lessons that we chose to come here for and not a bottle of sweet, old wine that makes you feel beautiful all the way . . . things start to look different! I have chosen a life that would be very challenging, I realise now. Looking back at the kind of experiences I chose only strengthens this fact further!

Today, at the age of 42, I realise that I came here to learn about the self worth, to value self as a beautiful, positive, constructive being. To accept myself as a person with a heart full of love and gratitude. To love myself for being the way I am. To look at myself with pride in the heart and a smile on the lips! *And to be able to learn all this, I planned a series of tough lessons.* I planned them right from my birth and they still are fully functional, so to speak! I arranged for a lot of opportunities and a possibility to learn this lesson, was available each time. It was one of the choices, to be honest. *The other choice was to sink in sorrow, feel worthless and invaluable, feel unappreciated and ignored and feel lost, frightened and lonely.* I see that I have chosen both, on different occasions.

And I asked the loving angels to be by my side, every time I went through a dark tunnel of challenges. And so they did, never failing me . . .

I could write a whole book about each angel of mine! I AM because THEY WERE THERE . . .

The first pair of angels decided to act as my parents till the time I grew into an adult. They took me under their wings at the age of 6 months and went on to protect me every which way.

I learnt to be patient, to help, to love selflessly, to be smiling in pain and to persist . . .

My first ever teacher in pre-primary school, was the second angel. She never disguised her fondness for me and laid the foundation of a positive life by showing complete trust in my abilities at that tender age. I have carried that feeling in my heart always. She was the first one I ran to, when I received the doctorate in psychotherapy and counselling. She had become very old by then. She looked at me with her eyes full of affection for me. She remembered my name and qualities as a five year old, even after a gap of 32 long years! I touched her feet and somehow managed to whisper through my chocked throat, "Ma'am, I am awarded the doctorate, the PhD." She pulled me close to her heart and kissed my forehead saying, "You are my goldmine. Keep shining bright and show others the way." Whatever confidence I have ever displayed till now, is a gift from her. I owe it to that one sentence in 1975 that I overheard from her conversation with another teacher! She had said, "Devayani is talented and can do many things ahead of her age."

The next one entered the scene at the age of 7 yrs. She was a girl a year younger to me who went on to become my best friend while growing up! She left me when I got married. Probably she was convinced that I no more needed her presence as I had a loved one to take care of myself.

In her presence, I learnt to share, to laugh, to rely, to feel nice about myself and to appreciate beauty . . .

A pair of handsome angels entered my life when I was about eight. In fact, I realise now that during that year, I suddenly got surrounded by many of them, I wonder why? Probably because they knew I would need support and protection the most then.

It was the same time when I experienced sexual abuse for the first time. My father touched my private parts after getting drunk. Most of the times, it was in the company of his friends. I loved the fact that my father was giving me exclusive attention which otherwise I would never get, yet at the same time I knew that something was wrong. I knew he shouldn't be touching so. I knew that I should not stand close to him when he calls me. But being close to him was too tempting all the same. A child needs parent's touch. Touch filled with affection and assurance. I wanted that too. And every time he called me close to him, I hoped I would get a pat on my back, a gentle peck on the cheeks, his hand stroking my head . . . it never happened. Finally, one of his much elder friends noticed it and asked him to stop immediately. I thank him in my heart, even today.

Those handsome angels became my heroes. They spoke to me, fed me my favourite snacks, encouraged me to become a good human being and constantly appreciated my talents. Though I never shared any of my embarrassing experiences with them, they seem to know that I was uncomfortable about something. They saw to it that I felt relaxed and happy in their company. They always made me laugh, the best thing that one human can give to another! They created a space so safe for me that I always longed to be with them. A never-ending source of unconditional love for me . . . That is what they both were to me.

When I was 10 yrs old, a man of my grandfather's age whom I was very fond of, kissed me. I was too deeply shocked by what was happening, frozen with disbelief that was enough not to react or to stop him. I hated the smell and the taste of his mouth and hated myself, holding myself responsible for his act. Though I was only lying down on the bed reading a story book, which I often did, I never did that ever again till I grew almost thirty . . . Though there was no provocation on my part, I still felt guilty.

The onset of my menarche was pretty early, at the age of ten, early by the general standards then. I handled it with a lot of confidence. My body had already started developing into a woman like one. It was at this time that a boy proposed to marry me! I, at 10, was not interested at all in him. But the concept that someone likes me and wants to spend his life with me caught on like wild fire. My imagination knew no bounds. I spent a lot of time thinking about my future husband-mostly an army commando in the olive green uniform! A smart, dashing, brave young man with a moustache! I loved this distraction no end and used it every time there was trouble around.

When I turned 12, I noticed being regularly watched by someone while taking bath. I got very conscious. Started taking more and more precautions and wondering who would it be. I found out one day that it was someone close to me, watching me in shower. I was filled with shame, anger, and embarrassment. I stopped talking to him. And then, he started touching me inappropriately. Every night, I would lie in my bed, with a blanket covering me from head to toe, heart beating louder than the drum. My eyes would be wide open inside the blanket, fully awake yet pretending to be asleep. I would suffocate, wanting to scream but could not, wanting to run away but could not, wanting to slap him but could not, wanting to request him not to do that ever again but . . . COULD NOT. My body would be stiff like a dried twig, unable to breath, unable to sleep, unable to speak. I did not know how to disclose this, whom to disclose this and what would happen next. Mother was already burdened by father's alcoholism and I did not want to bother

her further. Besides, I did not have a strong bond with her to have gone straightaway and shared it. So, this went on for almost six months. Finally, I somehow gathered enough courage to tell this to my mother and refused to sleep in the same room as his. She disbelieved me. She said I was mistaken. She said I was wrong. She said I was imagining. But I stuck to my words. I repeatedly told her what was happening. Somehow later, she spoke to that individual. I do not know what the conversation consisted of, but the incidence stopped after that. What an unfortunate way to lose someone who was close to my heart.

I reached the class 10th and my mother sent me to the math tuitions. The teacher, a bachelor in his late forties, was quite a well known person there. There were two girls and three boys studying with me. Within the first few meetings, I realised that he looked at me in a much different way than he did at other girls. He would keep staring at me with his big, round, glistening eyes. Then, on a Sunday morning, I went to the class as per the schedule only to realise that I was the only one there. He gave me a problem to solve, stood in front of me and started removing his clothes. An urgent sense of fright, flow of blood gushing to my head, heart beating at 250 decibels . . . I stood up when he started moving towards me, rushed out of the door that he had locked without my notice, locked it from outside and kept running till I reached my friend's house.

Coming back to the angels, the next one appeared when I was 18 . . . I used to feel extremely inferior, confused, perpetually tired and lost! I had stopped eating all together. I would drink water each time I felt hungry and that's about it. I was angry, fuming, disappointed, frightened all at the same time. One fine day, I found that I was unable to bend my legs. That frightened me further. I thought I had become incapacitated for life. I went to the Acupressure specialist and got myself cured over a couple of months. I learnt that I was suffering from a disease called 'marasmic kwashiorkor'; extremely malnourished children get this sometimes! And this is when he flew down to help me! He showed me the mirror. He showed me what I had within me. He helped me gather myself and stand upon my two feet. He trained me to set a target, focus upon it and put in 100% genuine efforts to achieve it.

He glorified my potential to such an extent that I was forced to make it come true! He encouraged me to perform to the best of my ability. He did everything that was actually needed to be done by my family members. He spent a lot of time to cheer me up, to push me ahead to perform and to win. He was a fabulous motivator and it did work! I earned a few trophies and many medals under his wings. I became an icon in the department and the university. All talked about me and my achievements. They followed my footsteps; they made me their role model. My name was written in golden letters on the board for all to see. I started to hope again.

All this while by the way, though I was nice and gentle to others, I did not give the same leverage to myself ever. I was very harsh with myself. I expected myself to handle situations with the wisdom of a hundred year old. I expected others to be irresponsible and for me to take the entire burden on my shoulders. I scored exceptionally high on nurturance, 97% to be precise, in the personality tests at the age of 22! I was constantly giving others what I longed for . . . I wanted to be nurtured, to be cared for, to be protected, to be supported, to be loved. And that is the time I realised that I still have a lot to experience, to gain and to feel!

In 1989, I met someone who most probably was my twin soul. I was going through an extremely rough patch in my life and I think that is the reason he walked in one fine morning!

My world began to look different. I became peaceful, calm, and joyous. The way I loved to describe it was to say that I was feeling LIGHT, BRIGHT AND RIGHT!! This was where I was accepted as I was, without a single bias or without any judgement. I was appreciated for my intentions, principles, thoughts and actions. My mind was full of melodious music and heavenly colours! I learnt in his presence that we have to decide what is nourishing to our souls and do those things over others!! I had the strength to face any obstacle in life. I was willing to face challenges and keep smiling along the way!

Surprisingly though, this was one of the most difficult times I was going through. I had lost my mother, the real one. I took a major decision of calling off my engagement to a person, whom other girls would have given anything to be with! My biological father refused to accept my decision and asked me never to enter his house ever again. At 19, I was a humiliated, rejected and alienated girl, yet very optimistic of my future and full of dreams, ambitions, aspirations . . . I somehow always felt protected by my angels. *I was alone but never lonely . . .*

The kind of personal growth that took place under the wings of this angel was mesmerising! The pace with which it happened was even more intriguing . . . as if the angel knew when to fly away, after making me brave enough to face the world!

I graduated in Human Development with good grades and took a post graduate diploma in hotel management. Worked very hard and bagged a good job after that. A very sincere, dedicated and skilled worker I came to be known as. I was happy, satisfied with myself and wanting more! So, after two years, I got back to school to get a masters' degree in Human Development. After a year, I lost my father, the real one. Now, I was really really alone. His death was a process of learning at a rather different level. I spent five days and nights with him, never leaving him for a moment. Neither did I eat nor sleep, sitting by his side, observing him sink and get delirious at times. I knew he didn't want to die. He wanted to be there for me, to protect me, to support me . . . But, he had to go and he didn't like it a bit. I kept on telling him to leave peacefully, not to worry about me, that I was able to look after myself . . . He would stare at me for hours, without blinking at times! It was overwhelming, it was draining, and it was frightening. Frightening because I could not control anything, I could not make it easier for him to cross the boundaries. On the last day, I lay next to him, just like I would when I was a little girl, placing my head on his thin, wrinkled arm and closed my eyes. All this while, I did not sleep a wink because I did not want him to go without my awareness. May be, somewhere inside, I was trying to control the process. MAY BE I WANTED TO CONTROL DEATH! But, this moment, I resigned and accepted that I should help him go beyond. May be my being awake stopped him from leaving me forever. So, I told him that he could leave whenever he wished and closed my eyes. It must have been for ten minutes and when I woke, he was gone.

Feeling happy for him, I went ahead with all the rituals that Hindu religion calls for. I was a girl and not allowed to even think in such a manner in the patriarchal system I grew up in! But I was adamant on doing all rites that a son performs for his father. After being ridiculed and shunned down by more than 20 Brahmins (priests), I met one real Brahmin who agreed to help me with this. He said that the emotions were more important than the gender and that my father was lucky to have a daughter like me . . . I brought his ashes home to perform a ritual on the 13th day.

While studying for the masters' degree, my guide suggested I conduct a research study on theatre and education. That is when I met another guardian angel of mine! In his presence, I was exposed to so many different facets of life that gave me tremendous insight into human mind and its functioning. I learnt from him that if one limits ones choices to what seems possible or reasonable, then one disconnects from what one truly wants . . . and what remains is only a compromise . . .! Each moment with him was a lesson learnt for keeps. He made me feel proud of what I was and aspire to become better each day. He taught me that people get lonely because they build walls within instead of the bridges! I grew up into an empathetic and mature professional just by observing him.

After getting married to the man I loved and giving birth to two beautiful angels of my own, I thought I did not need any more of angelic presence. Was I wrong? I sure was.

We all are born into a web of relationships and all of our learning, most of our happiness as well as misery stem from them. In fact, like J. Krishnamurti said, life is a process of relationship. As a human being, one cannot escape being related. Relationship is the basis of human existence and relationship has true significance if only it offers a process of self revelation.

I have always wondered as to what was the opposite of love. Would it be hatred, like we are made to believe? I never wanted to believe that though. And so, I kept on looking for the answer. And now, I have discovered that the answer is FEAR and not hatred. When we are not able to feel and express love, it is because some kind of fear is blocking us away. **Fear is the biggest obstacle in the path of love.** Fear is an unconscious refusal to face and move through our own pain. Fear creates pain in the body and to cover that pain up; we start using the crutches and get dependent /addicted to something. Those crutches could be food, music, TV, alcohol, drugs, relationships or another person . . . That is why after the initial euphoria ends, the bitterness, pain, guilt, and sorrow surfaces. Relationships by themselves do not cause pain and unhappiness. They, over a period of time, bring out what we already had within us, to the surface. All that was unresolved, all that we hoped that the other person will resolve, all that we believed that the other person will take us out of . . . In essence, all that we did not want to deal with, ourselves! All that we avoided all along! Everything that we tried to get distracted ourselves from.

I soon found myself talking to God and realised that I had to seek guidance for my soul.

There he was . . . waiting for me to remember him! He sent me a message to come see him. This angel taught me the procedure to connect with the universe. He showed me the way home, our real and permanent home. Under his guidance, my consciousness was transformed. From body – conscious, I became soul-conscious. It was as if I was drowning in the deep waters of disappointments and grief and he threw a lifeline of knowledge for me to fetch. I was saved one more time!

The path was unfamiliar and difficult to walk. My eyes were filled with tears. My legs felt weak and mind unsure of the results. Yet, I followed his directions. I had full faith in his words. I knew I was blessed to have met him. I was RIGHT!

In year 2000, yet another angel who changed my life at both, the gross and subtle level, charged into my life. A very pure soul himself, he taught me a technique using which I could look within, into the subconscious mind. It opened an entirely new chapter in my life wherein I could help myself as well as other people change lives at different levels immediately and permanently. I was so mighty impressed by this effective way of communicating with subconscious minds that I immersed myself into it. It has been 13 years now and I have a long list of souls that were empowered through me to lead improved lives. I am profusely grateful to this angel for guiding me in the right direction, for encouraging me to ask profound questions, for appreciating my effort and the way I faced adversities, for my intensity and intentions, for my urge to experience the entire spectrum of being human and above all, my desire to heal people. He taught me that action always generates inspiration, but inspiration seldom lead to actions . . . so, it is imperative to DO than to TALK!! He gave me courage to follow the truth no matter what!

I have shared my experiences of getting sexually abused with my readers here for two reasons. The first and the most logical one is that this book itself is about child sexual abuse and so, happens to be the most appropriate space to be written about. The second reason (which may not sound any rational or logical to most of us) is the strong urge to thank all those who helped me achieve my aim of understanding self worth. These are the souls who, now as I understand, must love me the most and therefore, agreed to provide opportunities for my growth, realisations and learning . . . I am convinced that they were a part of MY plan for this life on Earth and only played the role that WE all had drafted for each one of us to play here.

Though I have mentioned only a few individuals in this book, there have been many more, who tried to take advantage of my trust in them, in their humaneness. Many of them were known to me, and others were strangers. The range of abusive experiences was vast. That included every possible abusive gesture, from a lust filled touch to a forcible sexual intercourse against my protest, without my consent. ***It did not really matter if I knew them or not, as these experiences gave rise to identical feelings of being cheated, being used for ulterior motives, being targeted as an object that gives pleasure, being judged only by the physical appearance and not by what I am inside . . .*** These feelings pressurised me to put my foot down and stop the ongoing abuse. These feelings connected me with my innermost aim of realising that I am a valuable human being, capable of contributing to the welfare of humanity and healing pain. The same pain which I experienced all throughout. It was nothing but a reminder for me to go on and heal the same! Every time I felt complacent or started to engage in gross level, body conscious activities, I encountered something that brought me back to the soul conscious state, reminding to take an action at that level so that I could achieve my goal. How I cherish and respect this realisation now! Looking back, I can very clearly see the pattern of behaviour that I chose to practise. I was convinced that I was unable to say NO to anyone and I had to be nice to everyone. This behaviour at physical level attracted experiences that made me feel all the emotions mentioned earlier. With the blessings of my angels, I learnt how to put an end to such occurrences. I am really proud of myself today to know that never ever till date, did I let my subconscious go to sleep and let my conscious mind take over. I always stayed connected, no matter what. I have a strong sense of fulfilment to treasure for lifetime!!

Another extremely vital learning that occurred recently is about the dissociation with my own body and its consequences. I realise now that I disconnected from my body sometime while growing up because of the abusive experiences that I had then. I totally dissociated with my bodily needs and urges to an extent that it became unhealthy. I refused to fulfil the requirements on daily basis. I have already mentioned about the deficiency disorder I suffered from. I never tried to beautify my body with cosmetics, cloths, footwear, or any other thing that a girl of my age would do routinely. Moreover, I refused to accept any compliment for my appearance, no matter who paid it! This went on until a few days ago that while writing for this book, the fact dawned on me. Today, I am a renewed Devayani, accepting myself, as I am! It is only now that I have understood and then experienced the real meaning of my name: Devayani, the one who travels from darkness towards the light; the one who walks away from the ignorance towards knowledge!! Now, I look into the mirror and like what I see. I compliment self whenever appropriate! I can see that I have come a long way . . .

Healing as I understand now, begins as soon as the injury takes place. No matter whether the injury is on the body or in the mind, there is a system already in place and ready to go to work. When a child falls down while riding his bicycle and comes home with bleeding knees, the mother fixes it with medicines. Least realising that the wound begins to heal much before we take cognisance of its presence! A physical wound is treated by the body, the medicines are only a superficial modality, facilitating the healing process at times and becoming a hindrance in some situations.

As described by Voltaire, a famous French Enlightenment writer, historian and philosopher, the art of medicine consists in amusing the patient while nature cures the disease!!

Similarly, the psychological healing system gets automatically activated in the subtle, deeper layers of existence. How well the wound is healed depends upon how well connected the body and mind are! *If the criteria to be happy are to have our thoughts, words and actions moving in one direction, then to be healthy is to have our physical sensations and emotional states in synch!*

Each time I was faced with a crisis, I was willing to get rid of the life I planned, and embraced the life that was waiting for me with open arms! The kind of choices one makes decides the direction in which our life flows. No matter how many temptations were laid down on my way to wisdom, always chose the one that was humane. I did never flounder away from the principles of humanity. I always remembered that it is the easiest to fool self! Also experienced that on a couple of occasions, when I did not follow my inner guidance, I felt a loss of energy, loss of power and sense of spiritual numbness. Over a period of time, I judged that everything in life has a purpose.

Healing is a process of inner transformation. It is a path which while walking helps one reconstruct painful memories into lessons of life. It is a spontaneous process and comes naturally to us. Self realisation is one of the major consequences of healing. And most importantly, this is a self-sustaining system within each one of us living here! In fact, many a times, an intense crisis triggers the healing process in such a way that it facilitates resilience, maturity, and as a result, personal growth. But our anxieties, fears and countless layers of social conditioning often create a one way window in our mind through which we can only look outside instead if within. Over a period, we lose touch with our inner self. *This is when our screams turn silent* . . .

Most of us like to believe that when the box of painful experiences is full, we must close it, sit on the lid and fake a smile to the world! We like to believe that this is what healing means! I too was at this juncture once wherein I practised faking a smile! But the real healing begins when one opens that box with courage, takes out painful experiences one by one, turn them into an empty memory by rendering it without any power of emotion, and when the box is finally empty, close it, look into the mirror and smile facing yourself . . .

Somebody said that in the wake of difficult times, the best revenge is to live our life well . . .

I feel that by giving our best to the life, accepting human limitations, striving to find out the aim of our life and making that dream come true, understanding who you really are, and offering love and care to ourselves, it is possible to live a worthwhile, meaningful life . . .

And off course, we always have our guardian angels to hold the little finger and show us the way! They meet us as people who demonstrate courage, strength, tenderness and a huge capacity to love. In turn, we learn to survive, sustain, heal and grow . . .

"We are born alone, we live alone and we die alone. Only love and friendship can create an illusion of not being alone . . ." There was a time in my life when I would agree totally with this statement. But my angels made me see the other side of reality. Today, I am very sure that I shall never be left alone to struggle here by my guardian angels. They will always appear whenever I need them. They will always be with me when I call out for their help. I love them all and I wish that all those reading this page, get to meet their own angels soon!

ACKNOWLEDGEMENT

W E VALUE PEOPLE IN OUR LIFE ON TWO OCCASSIONS . . . before getting them . . . . . . and after losing them! But I am fortunate to have had valuable people in my life and want to share my gratitude towards them all. I strongly believe that all experiences are significant, planned by none other than oneself! Therefore, I want to especially thank all those, who presented me with challenges, created obstacles in my growth and progress, triggered painful and unfair moments . . . because while reflecting, I do marvel that without their contribution, how could I ever have known my own potential, strengths and will power? Yes, I did face all of those challenges with hundred percent optimism, zest, enthusiasm and self-confidence.

My husband, Wing Commander S Kashyap, VM and both my sons, Manavendra and Anshumaan, gave me all the strength to go through the tough times and stood there shining in the darkest of my nights, like a lighthouse!

I am indebted to the Balboa press (Hay House Publications) for giving me an international platform to reach out to more than many around . . .

And yes, I am grateful to the little girl inside, who coaxed me to take up this topic for research and give justice to her own bruised childhood memories. She belonged to the category that keeps getting up saying 'thank you' every time she is punched down. I learnt to love and forgive from her!! She is the one who made me realise that love has never been her decision. It is a choice that she always preferred. And in the thought that, LOVE IS NOT ONLY SOMETHING THAT YOU FEEL . . . IT IS SOMETHING THAT YOU DO!

ABOUT THE AUTHOR

B orn and educated in Mumbai, India. Family inheritance of quest for knowledge, justice, culture, and adventure. A strong urge to understand Human Development led to a doctorate degree in psychotherapy and counselling. While studying, participated in a variety of cultural and adventurous activities and was adjudged All India Best Cadet as well as University All Round Best Cadet in the National Cadet Corps. It was during same time that a deep sense of connection as well as responsibility towards the environment developed. While working as a freelance mental health therapist in various cities, developed a keen interest in Neuro- psychology. Her efforts to spread awareness about mental health and help people cope with their lives better have continued. The title 'pearl of Hyderabad' was conferred upon by JCI International (worldwide federation of young leaders and entrepreneurs) in 2007, towards extraordinary contribution to the field of Graphology and mental health. Has successfully treated adults and children for conditions like depression, suicidal tendencies, anxiety, panic attacks, sexual abuse, asthma and a variety of phobias. As a consultant psychotherapist, has been conducting encounter groups for couples and adolescents, interactive workshops on sexuality education, 'I am safe', a training program for girls on physical and psychological defence, divergent thinking. She teaches certification courses in Handwriting Analysis. As an independent researcher, the author has presented a no of research papers in the National as well as International conferences. Her expertise in psychotherapeutic techniques such as Art therapy, Graphotherapy, REBT, Core somatic Integration and

D S Kashyap, PhD.

Humanistic modalities has led many individuals towards personal growth and better coping. Research interest in subconscious mind continues to fascinate self. The author currently lives with her husband and two sons in Mumbai, India.

BIBLIOGRAPHY

Kellogg, Nancy. Clinical Report—The Evaluation of Sexual Behaviors in Children. Published online August 31, 2009 Pediatrics Vol. 124 No. 3 September 1, 2009 pp. 992 -998.

Andreessen N C (1998) The crisis in clinical research: Editorial comment, American Journal of Psychiatry, 155-160

Spielberg (2002) Personality traits revealed in handwriting analysis.

McGrath (1994). When feeling bad is good, ed.2. 34-36

Conway, (1987) Instant people reading through handwriting, Pauls press, New Delhi

Gupta, C.B. (1997) An introduction to statistical methods (8th edi) Pearl Offset Press, New Delhi-15

Hollander, P.S. (2003) Handwriting analysis. Jaico Publishing House, M.G Road, Mumbai-400 001

Rajore, M.J. (2001) The Write Stuff, vol.1, Raj Printers, Kasba Peth, Pune-11

Rajore, M.J. (2002) The Write Stuff, vol.2, Raj Printers, Kasba Peth, Pune-11

Burman, KS. (1988) Childhood Years, St.Paul Society, Allahabad

Handbook of Child Psychology, 4th edi, vol.3 Cognitive Development, John Wiley and Sons, New York

Suzy Ward, (1996) Indicators of sexual abuse in handwriting, Journal of the American society of Professional Graphologists, vol.4, 35-55

Amend Karen, and Ruiz, Mary (1990). Handwriting analysis. Newcastle publ.

Brush, loyal. (1985). Handwriting analyst's handbook. Overland park, Kansas

Koren, Anna. (1887) A Comprehensive Guide To Handwriting Analysis. New York, NY: Adams Books

Link, Betty. (1987) Advanced Graphology. Northbrook IL.

Mestler, Mary. (1985) Letters of the alphabet. Pittsburgh

Nezos, Renna. (1986). Graphology: the interpretation of handwriting. Scriptor books, London

Ellingham-Jones, Patricia (1989). Successful women, their health and handwriting. PWJ Publ, Tehama, CA.

Kashyap, Devayani (2012). Anuttarit. Power Publ, Kolkata, India.

Aschaffenburg, Karl. (1986). Collected essays on various aspects of handwriting examination, Princeton, New Jersey

Naftali, Ari. (1988).Behavior factors in handwriting identification, the journal of criminal law, criminology and police science, vol.4, 56

Siegel, P (1988) American left handed writings. Experiencing graphology, Freund Publ, London

Anastasi, A; Urbina, S (2005) psychological testing. 7th edi. Pearson Edu, Singapore

Chew, J (1988). Women survivors of childhood sexual abuse. The Haworth press, New York

Baldwin, M.W. (1987). Journal of personality and social psychology, vol.52, 1087-1098

Briere, John (1996) Child and schema of sexual abuse, National Center for PTSD, NCP Clinical Quarterly, 6(2)

Virani, Pinky (2001). Bitter chocolate: child sexual abuse in India, New Delhi

Faller, Cathleen (1995). Evaluating children suspected of having been sexually abused. Sage Publn

Sharma, B.R.; Gupta, Manisha (2004) Child abuse in Chandigarh and its implications Journal of clinical forensic medicine, vol.11 (5), 248-256

SRIJAN (Sexual and Reproductive Health Network for Jointaction) http://www.yrshr.org/stat_builder/view_data.asp

EXPERT REVIEW: 1

t is universally acknowledged that the Indian society is going through a phase of acute crisis. The inherited institutions are falling apart. Dr D. S. Kashyap has so aptly highlighted the addressing of pressing issues related to child abuse. The underlying malaise that defines the very foundation of the evil in the society has been so aptly portrayed and presented by Dr. Kashyap for us to sit up and take notice of. Perhaps for the first time the correlation between the post-traumatic stress symptoms and presence of the grapho-indicators for the child sexual abuse has been studied in such minute detail. It is to her singular credit that her efforts have brought up a plethora of possibilities for treatment and enforcement of correctional practices of such devious acts.

Mr. Anal Pandit
Director,
Institute of Graphological Research
Mumbai, India.

EXPERT REVIEW: 2

T he study has been done in depth considering all the parameters. This book highlights genuine graphological distortions due to affected mindset very beautifully. The author has made a commendable effort in reflecting a child's grievances to the core. She has authentically endeavoured to portray sexually abused child's feelings effectively. With every passing page, you feel the pain and agony of the abused. She connected this science with the mindset efficiently keeping a child's sufferings as her focus. The crux of the book is the way she has thrown light on the children subjected to abuse in our society.

Mr. Millind Rajore.

Director

Institute Of Graphology and Personal Success

505, 5th Floor, West Wing, Aurora Towers,

M. G. Road, Pune- 411001

Maharashtra, India.

Tel: +91-020 40068757, 26124974,

+91-9325455758

Website:www.mjrajore.com, mjrajore.wordpress.com/

E-mail : igpspune@yahoo.com, Facebook.com/MJRajore

EXPERT REVIEW: 3

I t is a taboo to talk about sex and more so about sexual abuse in our country, India. More difficult is to acknowledge that sexual abuse happens daily of children, including infants. However, it is a subject of great community concern and focus of many professional and legal initiatives. Of late, we have seen the media showing increased coverage of sexual abuse including cases of rape and murders by people of repute and family members of those abused.

The author has very aptly named her book on detection of child sexual abuse through handwriting as "Silent Screams". In most cases the screams of the child remain silent. The parents are also mute even after disclosure about abuse as the first reaction is that of disbelief and rejection.

Proving sexual abuse is very difficult as the only witness is the child who is abused, and the statement of the abused is not always believed. The only evidence is indirect and there is high degree of suspicion. 40 to 50% of children in the age group of 11 to 17 years studied in this study had some form of sexual abuse. Any deviation from normal behaviour in a normal child should raise the suspicion of sexual abuse. Early detection is the key. And the simplest answer to the key is handwriting analysis. The author has very clearly shown that handwriting analysis can indicate personality traits and grapho-indicators associated, commonly found in the abused population and uncommon/absent in the non-abused population. It was also found that even the degree, mild, moderate or severe can be detected by handwriting analysis with good degree of accuracy.

The author has very well described about sexual abuse, its incidence, causes, the effects and the social consequences. The study has abundant number of real life cases of child sexual abuse by family, friends, and strangers. These cases describe the helplessness of the victim and how their life was affected negatively as older children or adults. A child who is the victim of prolonged sexual abuse usually develops low self-esteem, a feeling of worthlessness and an abnormal or distorted view of sex. The child may become withdrawn and distrustful of adults, and can become suicidal. Most of them could have benefited if early intervention was done. This study has very well described the role of parents, the doctors, psychological counsellors, school counsellors and the books written by the academicians in preventing and managing the sexually abused child.

For a solution to be found, one has to be aware that there is a problem. The eyes do not see what the mind does not know. For a good solution, problem has to identify early and fast. I compliment Dr. Kashyap for taking up this unusual but very important study. I am sure this work will help the people to sensitize them about the occurrence of child abuse in the society. I would recommend this to be read by parents, teachers, police and all those concerned with the well being of the children and community at large.

"Love is an expression of power. We can use it to transform our world."

Dr. Sanjeev Goel
M.D. (Pediatrics)
President Elect, Academy of Pediatrics, Gujarat
Executive Board Member, Indian Academy of Pediatrics, Mumbai (2014)
Email: goelsanjeev@gmail.com
Phones:
+91-265-2582516(h)
+91-9825265114(m)

HANDWRITING SAMPLE: 1

'amusing park.' Gardens etc. well my family and went out of station and I enjoy very much. My sisters are good and loves me very much and I also love them very much. I obey my mummy papa and my elders very much and in school teachers. I am very emotional thats why my friend won't allow me to cry. I cried in everything but not everytime. In my colony I play with my friend a lot. We play so many things and enjoy it. I love my parents, friends so very much. I don't like animals specially dogs, cats. I like birds all the birds. I love them.

ANNEXTURE 1B

HANDWRITING SAMPLE:2

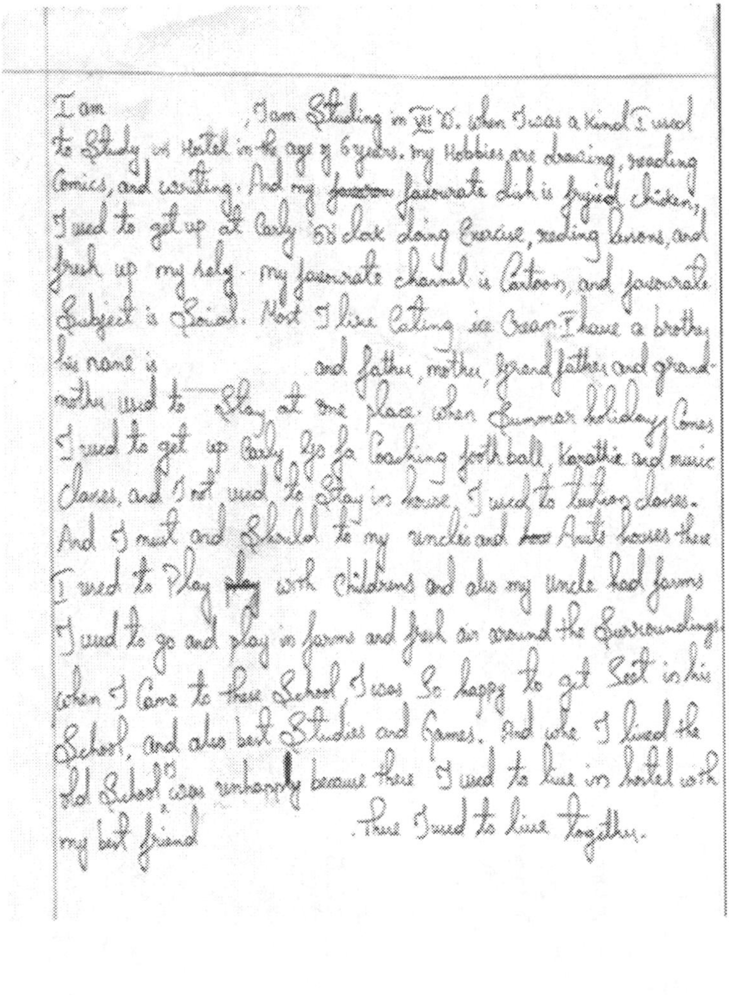

I am , I am Studing in XII D. when I was a Kind I used to Study in Hostel in the age of 6 years. my Hobbies are drawing, reading Comics, and writing. And my ~~favour~~ favourate dish is fryied chicken, I used to get up at early 5 o clock doing Exercise, reading lessons, and fresh up my selv. my favourate channel is Cartoon, and favourate Subject is Social. Next I like Eating ice Cream. I have a brother his name is and father, mother, grand father and grand-mother used to Stay at one place. when Summer holidays Comes I used to get up early go for Coaching foot ball, Karathie and music classes, and I not used to Stay in house, I used to tution classes. And I must and Should to my uncles and ~~two~~ Auts houses there I used to Play ~~play~~ with childrens and also my uncle had farms I used to go and play in farms and fresh air around the Surroundings. when I Came to these School I was So happy to get Seat in his School, and also best Studies and Games. And when I lived the old School I was unhappy because there I used to live in hostel with my best friend . There I used to live together.

ANNEXTURE 1B

HANDWRITING SAMPLE:3

...my friend are very good because they study good, and they do not tease anymore. We play games very nice, and we distribute our fruit to our classmates and I like all subjects very much and I love science very much, and because I want to become scientist and I have learn about what how animal are born and I my family is my father is a conductor, and my mother is a clerk in a bank. In private and Sind Bank, and my big brother is a mechanical engineer and my big sister is doing doctor. ... roots, and my hobby is to play computer games, and watching t.v. and listening radio songs, and to play any other games like football, basketball, cricket, kabaddi and no-cow ball and cut etc. and I have forgot to ...

HANDWRITING SAMPLE: 4

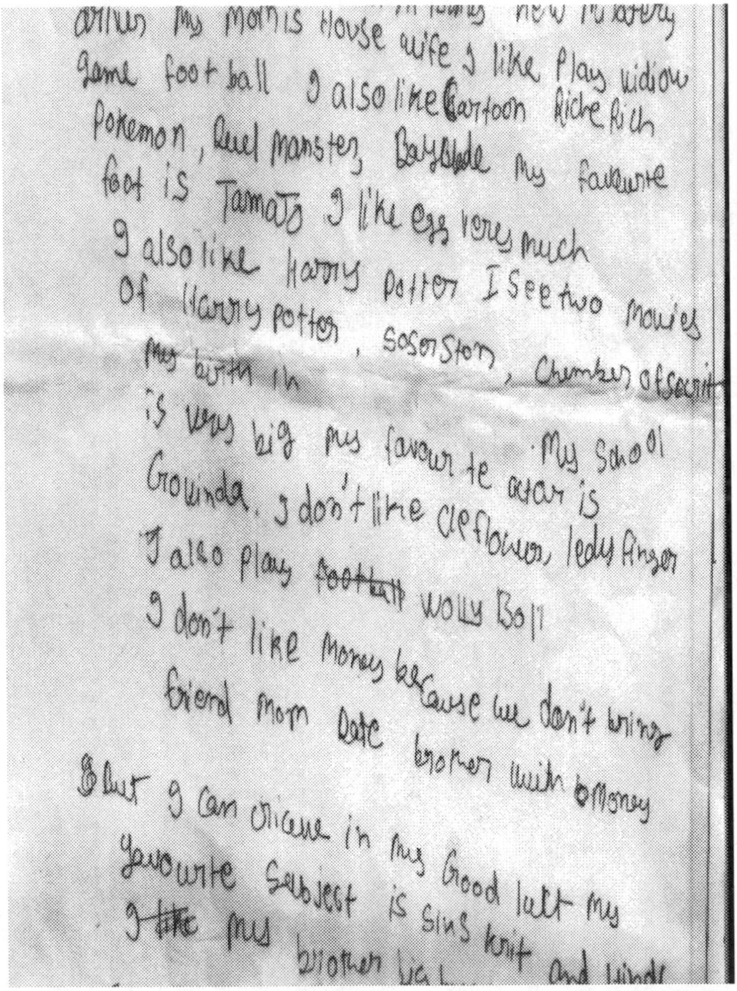

HANDWRITING SAMPLE: 5

brothers and no sister. we bout I like to play, read the bo
and sing song . In our .. holedays we will go to play
in the morning . My fathers, name is v. Prakash has
my mothers name is Anita and my brothers na
is V. Dhananjay - I dont like to eat Idlidos .

I our school . Ihave may friends ish our St
I have . B my friends friends will
come to my house and we will play
I and my best friend shoeth will go
to play a ride on her his . bicle . I
have one cycle and many brother has
one School my friend has two bickys
and . one active and one two cars. we wil
go to internal hope and we will play there and
like more to play video games but I dont ha
my parane subject is english and social
I like doing drawing and we dont
have phone but we dont are going
to bey a mobile . My father with

HANDWRITING SAMPLE: 6

hobbies are watching TV, playing, studying etc. I
am a very kind student. I love my school very
much and I have many friends. They are
very good and kind to me. I enjoy to share my
secrets with my family members. My golden time
which I hadn't forget till today was that the
appreciation of my principal when I am in LKG.
My embaracing time when my mother scolded me in
my front of my brother cousin. My Grandparents
they are so nice they will give lots of love to me.
I love my grandparents more than my parents. I have
an ambition to become a expert in any of course by but

HANDWRITING SAMPLE:7

in Railways. & I like computer games. My hobbies are playing, studying, watching & T V etc. I want to become a doctor. and treat the poor without cost. I like Hyderabad because it has a good and cool climate. I like my friends very much and they too like me very much. I want the world to be in harmony and I don't like war and destructive weapons because they destroy human life, plants, animals etc. I like reading books like science fiction and biographies. I want a dog but my parents do not allow me to keep it. I don't like wearing shoes as they bite my legs. I like milk and curd very much. I don't like bags weighing much. as they my shoulders pain. I want science & Technology to be useful and not as destructive weapons. I am afraid of the dark. If I would be a like superman I would save everybody.

HANDWRITING SAMPLE: 8

reading ...
carrot Halwa and panipuri . my favorite festival is
sun sankranti and diwadi adro . I like to go for
ride with motor cycle . My Best friend is
adey . He share food with me and share some books
also . my favorite teacher is Smith mam . she is
a english teacher . my father is a business man
my father mother is a house wife
my brahor is studing in trier Second yearBpc
I want to become a pilot officer
my father gives me a 50 ruppes every month
of last date it is my pocket money. Even
I have a big family in my father village.
my favorite program is tom & Jerry. I am
collecting every month 50 ruppes and putting in
pretty bonk because to by a playsation. In my

Graphology training around the world

Training in Europe:

Four academic institutions around the world currently offer an accredited degree in handwriting analysis.

- The University of Urbino, Italy: MA (Graphology)
- Instituto Superior Emerson, Buenos Aires, Argentina: BA (Graphology)
- Centro de Estudios Superiores (CES) Buenos Aires, Argentina: BA (Graphology)
- Autonomous University of Barcelona, Barcelona: Spain: MA (Graphology)
- Université de Paris, Paris: France: MA (Graphologie)

Training in the United States:

New School for Social Research, New York, diploma in Graphology. Graphology track Associate Arts Degree, Felician College, in Lodi, NJ. Within the United States, graphology education in 2011 is primarily provided via correspondence courses available from accrediting agencies like the International Graphoanalysis Society (IGAS) in Kensington, Pennsylvania.

D S Kashyap, PhD.

Training in India:

Institute Of Graphology and Personal Success
505, 5th Floor, West Wing, Aurora Towers,
M. G. Road, Pune- 411001
Maharashtra, India.
Tel: +91-020 40068757, 26124974,
+91-9325455758
Website :www.mjrajore.com, mjrajore.wordpress.com

Institute of Graphological Research
B-404, Vaibhav Apartments, Behind Gammon India,
Next To VIP Lounge, Old Prabhadevi Road,
Prabhadevi,
Mumbai – 400025
Maharashtra, India.
+91-**9869535481**
(022) 24228836

www.graphologyinstitute.net
www.graphologyinstitute.com

LIST OF TABLES

SERIAL NO	TITLE	PAGE NO
1	Objectives of the study	42
2	Outcome of phase 1	44
3	Description of sample	45
4	Negative traits	52
5	Emotional interactions with primary caregiver	67

ANNEXTURE 1E

LIST OF FIGURES